BUILDING CHAMPIONS

COACHING, PARENTING, AND PLAYING TO WIN IN WHAT REALLY MATTERS

CHRIS M. STEWART

Building Champions by Chris M. Stewart
Published by Chris M. Stewart
Athens, OH 45701
https://chrismstewart.com

For permissions contact: cstewart1993@gmail.com.

Cover photo by Trisha Smathers Photography: smathersphotography@yahoo.com.

ISBN-10: 1986508684
ISBN-13: 978-1986508681

CONTENTS

INTRODUCTION

This is the book I wish I would have read before I began mentoring young lives through coaching. It's the book that I wish someone would have handed to me before I had my own children. It's the book that I could have benefited from before our family ventured out into the world of travel ball. Don't get me wrong, we loved every minute of it and are very grateful for all the wonderful experiences we have had through being a sports family. Yet, there are too many moments when I wish I could have a do-over.

We don't get do-overs in real life. All we get is the opportunity to learn from our failures and then try to help others to not make the same mistakes. That's why I am thankful you have this book in your hand. Whether you are a coach, a parent, or a young athlete, I had you in mind as I wrote. If you are a parent and also a coach, I especially had you in mind. If you are a parent who coaches your own kids, then you are the perfect storm!

According to the Open Access Journal of Sports Medicine, three out of four American families with school-aged children have at least one child playing an organized sport—a total of about 45 million kids. By age 15, as many as 80% of these kids have quit.[1]

Maybe they lose interest. Maybe parents lose perspective and create excessive expectations, causing their children to choose hobbies with less pressure and less stress. For some of the 80 percent, maybe the problem isn't due to losing interest or parental pressure, but maybe the problem is coaches. Maybe there is just a systemic problem with the entire culture of youth sports.

Plain and simple, the world needs better coaches. Coaches are arguably the most important and influential people in the life of another person. We need more men and women to embrace this critical role, but who more importantly understand the big picture and can relate it to their players. We need more parents who do not lose their minds for ten or so years while their children are playing organized sports. We need more young athletes who understand the greatest value of playing sports is learning how to become a champion in the game of *life*.

In the summer of 2011, I was coaching a 12U travel baseball team, the Athens Attack, which my 12-year old son was a member. In one particular tournament, our team had lost a game pretty badly, and my son had one of those days. You know what I mean. He didn't have his good stuff. It was an off-day (or more like an *awful* day). After it was over, we had no sooner clicked our seatbelts inside the car and I immediately started in on him. I pointed out everything he did wrong. I called him out for his lack of hustle. I made comments about how much his mother and I sacrifice and invest so that he could play on a summer travel team, and how disappointing it is to see that his effort was not matching our commitment and sacrifice for him. Oh, it was a real kicker of a speech, let me tell you. Fifteen minutes later (which probably felt more like fifteen hours to my son), we pulled into the hotel parking lot and I was finally done berating him. Before we got out of the car, I concluded my little diatribe with something like, "You know that I only say these things because I love you and want what is best for you, right?" He nodded his head and we got out of the car.

Shortly after we had unpacked our gear into our hotel room, he asked if we could go down to the swimming pool. I said, "Sure, you go ahead. I'll be down in a little bit." For the next few moments, while I was alone in that hotel room, something hit me. It was like a wave of emotion that I couldn't stop, because I didn't see it coming. I replayed in my mind the entire car ride from the ballpark to the hotel, only this time I was in his seat. I was the 12-year old kid. I had forgotten what that was like. Somewhere along the way I forgot that kids play ball because it is fun and because it gives them the chance to develop great friendships.

Eventually, I composed myself and walked down to the pool but stood back at a distance and just watched. An entire team of boys laughing, doing canon-balls into the water, splashing, playing chicken, and having the time of their lives. If I were to ask my son today if he could tell me what our 12U record was, or even how many championships we won that summer, I'd be willing to bet he has no recollection whatsoever of those answers, and that is certainly not because he doesn't love the game of baseball.

It's just that, those things are not the most important things. What are the most important things? That is what this book is about. It's about family. It's about coaching. It's about being a great teammate and discovering what it takes to be a champion. When our goal is to be champions—not merely win championships but *be champions*, there is a difference—then it means we approach things a little differently in our coaching, playing, and parenting.

Not everyone will have the opportunity to win a championship in their lifetime. It is just not something that is totally within a person's control. A lot of external factors have to go your way in order to win a championship. But every person—every mom, dad, son, daughter, and coach—can *become a champion.* There is a difference.

One quick thing I'd like to add about the structure of the book. You will notice it is grouped into three parts: The Coach, The Player, The Parent. If you would prefer, you can skip directly to the section that best describes you. However, I would encourage you to read the other sections as well, because to be honest, there is something in each section that is relevant for everyone. Plus, we become even better at our own role in life when we better understand the roles and perspectives of others.

So, whether you are a coach, a player, or a parent, I hope you will get something out of this book. If I had a time machine, I would turn it back to when my kids were 7-years old and I would make myself read this. That is how much I believe in the message that is contained in these pages. Since I can't go back and have a do-over, I humbly offer these lessons to you. Together, let's build some champions!

PART I

THE COACH

"A good coach can change a game. A great coach can change a life."

—John Wooden

1

CALL ME COACH

I have been called a lot of names over the years, probably more than I even realize. Most people call me Chris. My kids call me Dad. Friends in school called me Stew or Stewie. I have been called Mr. Stewart. I have been called Pastor, Preacher, and Teacher.

Of all the various names I have been known by over the years, one of the names I have treasured dearly is the name "Coach." If you have ever been called Coach, then maybe you understand. If you don't understand, then I am glad you are reading this book. My aim is to help you discover an element of coaching that, in my opinion, should not only be at the top of our list of goals to accomplish, but it should be the very force that drives everything we do, say, and teach. It should be our primary mission.

If you are not a coach, have never been a coach, or have no intentions of ever coaching, don't go away just yet. You may actually be a coach and not even realize it. Or, you may be placed in a position of leadership where the skills you will be required to have are that of a coach. Yes, we're going to address some things in this book that pertain specifically to coaching sports, but what I am most interested in is *life*. Everyone in life needs a coach. Therefore, I would suggest that there is perhaps no more important person on the planet today than Coach.

Former NFL 1st round draft pick, Perry Tuttle, says that "coaches today are the fishermen of Jesus' day."[2] What a powerful statement! Jesus actively sought out and chose twelve men to be his disciples. Many from among the first of those chosen were fishermen. They were chosen because they could be trusted to carry out and pass along the life-changing message that he came to give the world. Likewise, today, coaches are the most likely people to impact and bring clarity to the most important issues of life, if they are intentional about it and if they understand that is in fact the most significant aspect of their role.

I didn't always understand this. For the first 20 years of my coaching career, I saw my role as preparing people to accomplish a task. My relationship with my players was based on what they could do to help accomplish the task. Every interaction with them, every conversation, and every coachable moment was spent focusing on the tasks at hand. Sure, I would sometimes say things like, "This skill will serve you well later in life," but I did not show genuine interest in their lives outside of the context of the sport we were involved in together.

In today's world, perhaps more than ever, I believe every person on the planet needs a coach. Every person needs someone in their life who plays the role of Coach. For those of you who already fulfill the role of Coach, please take a moment to contemplate the depth of influence you have on the people you are leading and mentoring. There is so much more going on, every day, than just the X's and O's and your instruction of the game.

The high school baseball team I coached had a really great photographer who followed us throughout our season and into our post-season tournament run. After the 2017 season, I was looking through her photo catalog and I came across this one photo that was taken shortly after our final game of the season had ended. In the front of the shot are two of our assistant coaches embracing two of our senior players, all in tears. In the back of the photo is me embracing my son, also a senior player. My back is to the camera, which means you can only see his face, but I will admit that mine was also red and puffy-eyed, as we too were shedding plenty of tears.

It has been said that a picture is worth a thousand words. Whenever I look at that picture, my heart fills up with so much more than just a thousand words. In fact, I still have difficulty looking at that photo without my eyes beginning to water. It wasn't just that the picture was taken after the last game of our season, a historic baseball season for our high school: undefeated league champions, Sectional champions, District champions, and one game away from a State semifinal appearance. It was also the last game I would ever again coach my son. It was the last game in which that particular senior class and I would ever be on the field together, after being together since they were eight years old.

A lifetime of coaching, and that photo was taken the moment we all realized it was complete. It was over.

Maybe a fraction of the emotions depicted in the photo were because we had lost the Regional Championship game. Perhaps that was part of it, but for me (and I suspect for all those other young men and coaches), it was much more than that. It was appreciation. It was respect. It was love.

Friends, that is what coaching is about. *Loving* people. And loving them enough to give them what they need most. If we miss those opportunities, then we aren't coaching. We are just instructors of a game. We are just teaching principles. We are just bosses who oversee a task. But a *coach* provides an equal balance of love and accountability, teaching discipline and instilling wisdom every day you are together.

"Coach" is without any doubt in my mind the most important role on the planet today. In an ever-changing world, one constant can be the voice and the presence of *Coach*. Do not ever take that for granted.

2

_____

THE MOST VALUABLE QUALITY OF COACHING

Here is a question for you. When answering, go with your first instinct, the first response that pops into your mind.

Which is more important?

    A.   Coaching your sport

    B.   Coaching people

Some of you right now are saying, "But Chris, there needs to be an option C: Both." I intentionally did not include an option C. Of course, both types of coaching *are* important. I am not going to deny that, but I want you to think about which is *more* important. The fact is, your answer to that question will teach you a lot about your coaching and particularly what motivates you and what drives you as a coach. Your answer is directly linked to your "why." Namely, *why do you coach?*

If I were to ask this question to my 30-year old self, I would have undeniably chosen answer A. Coaching the sport of baseball was the most important thing to me, without a doubt. I was determined to make whatever team I coached the most fundamentally sound team around. We didn't waste a single minute on anything that didn't have to do with getting better offensively or defensively. Practice plans were filled every day with hitting, fielding, pitching, catching, base running, bunting, and situational strategy. I prided myself in knowing the game and in coaching the game, in my words, *the right way*.

When I was coaching *the game*, the players mattered primarily in the sense that they helped accomplish the goals of the game. I insisted that every player respect the game, and I would constantly remind them that the game is much bigger than they, and that the game will be around for much longer after they are gone. For 30-year old me, everything was about *the game*, and the game was everything.

Now, I am not suggesting that any of those things are bad. Many of those things are still true for me. I still put as much emphases on fundamentals and strategy, as all we who coach sports should. I just want to share with you how 45-year old Coach Stewart has come to differ somewhat from 30-year old Coach Stewart. Something pretty significant has changed in my approach.

When I first began coaching (baseball) I was 22 years old. I had just finished playing the game and still had a lot of passion for it, a lot of love for it, and an intense thirst to want to remain involved in the game. So, I felt like coaching would be the perfect opportunity for me to be able to quench that thirst. As a first-time coach of a 15U team, I decided that I would put together a "Manual" for the players on the team and also for the parents to be able to know a little more about me, my coaching philosophy, and how our team was going to play the game.

Over the years I have continued to utilize a Team Manual, but like my coaching, that manual has evolved quite a bit. In the early days, it was primarily an X's and O's book—hitting mechanics, fielding fundamentals, pitching mechanics, offensive strategy, bunt defenses, double-steal plays, cut-off and relay procedures—you get the picture.

Today's manual still includes all of those X' and O's pages, but now there are twice as many pages. The newer pages deal with mental strength, developing character, the power of positive energy and *giving* energy versus being an energy vampire, how to approach difficult situations and adversity, how to develop trust among teammates, how to be the best teammate possible, and many more skills they will need. Yes, these skills will be needed on the baseball diamond, but they will also be needed in the classroom, in their friendships, in their careers, and in their marriages.

So, which coaching philosophy is more important to me today? Without any doubt, it's answer B, coaching *people*. If this is your foundation for coaching, it will be the firmest and strongest of any other foundation. Your team and your *people* who make up your team, will be built to last. They will succeed in more than just between the lines of the ball diamond, field or court.

The above graphic illustrates exactly how I perceive this. You will notice that one word in the graphic is much larger than the other word in the graphic. Obviously, LIFE is so much bigger than BALL. This is fundamentally true on so many levels. I've seen a t-shirt design from one of the leading athletic apparel brands which used the slogan, "Ball is life!" My answer to that is, no. It really isn't. I know that's just a slogan, and some people might say, "Gosh, lighten up Stewart!" But I believe words matter, and that t-shirt slogan sells because it's really how many people feel, unfortunately.

Here's the reality. Life is going to come at each one of our players pretty hard someday after there is no more ball. When it does, they will need to lean on something sturdier than how to field a ground ball, improve their spin rate, increase their exit velocity and get the perfect launch angle.

When life comes at them hard, will they be able to lean on something you taught them or modeled for them while they were playing under your coaching? When this is the attitude that creates our mindset and approach, it changes the way we coach. In my opinion, it makes us a *better* coach. It revolutionizes the way we coach!

There are basically two kinds of coaches. Coaches whose focus is on helping the team win, and coaches whose focus is on helping the team be the best they can be. One is a narrow, short-sighted focus. The other is a broad, wide-ranging focus. One type of coach uses the players to achieve something in the sport. The other type of coach uses the sport to achieve something in the players.

John Wooden said that you would not find a single person that he had coached who ever heard him mention *winning*. Wooden was one of the winningest and most accomplished men to ever coach the game of basketball. Yet, he is remembered more for his definition of *success*, which he left behind for all of us who desire to achieve what he had achieved: "Success is peace of mind, which is a direct result of self-satisfaction in knowing you did your best to become the best you are capable of becoming."

When I consider the implications for coaches who desire to live by that philosophy and implement Coach Wooden's definition of success, this is how I think we can accomplish it. *Don't focus on winning a championship. Focus on building champions.* We all know that only one team gets to win a championship at the end of the year. That is not always within your control. To win a championship, the reality is, a lot of uncontrollable factors have to go your way. However, having a team full of champions year in and year out *is* possible. It is within your control, and it is what makes it all worth it, year in and year out!

What does this mean, and how is it accomplished? It means that for the greatest coaches in the world, the emphasis is *people*, not *product*. The goal is *becoming*, not *arriving*. The focus is on the *process*, not the *outcome*. The reward is a life that has been impacted in such a positive way that he or she wants to carry on the example that he or she learned from you. That is a reward that doesn't collect dust behind a glass case. That is a reward that has life, and gives life to countless others for many years to come.

This, in my opinion, is the most valuable aspect of coaching.

Now, for anyone who refused to answer the question at the beginning of this chapter because you were looking for an option C (coaching both), I will address that briefly. I believe when a coach's priority is answer B (coaching people) then it makes answer A (coaching the sport) a whole lot easier, and a whole lot more fun. When our priority is the *person*, then that relationship-based focus will take the implementation of fundamentals to a whole new level. Your passion for wanting to instill greatness in your players will be significantly higher. Your focus and preparation will be more precise. And everyone's love for the game will increase noticeably.

The beauty of coaching is, you don't have to just focus on one or the other. However, which one you prioritize will certainly determine the kind of coach you are and in large part, the kind of people your players are going to be after they are no longer under your tutelage.

3

———————

COACHING THE PERSON

The idea of *coaching the person* is such an important one that I felt it could use its own chapter. I would like to go a little deeper in explaining exactly what I mean by coaching the "person" first. Then, secondary to coaching the person, we can focus on coaching *the player*.

Regardless of the sport or endeavor, I have discovered that if I can help *the person* to get in a good place first—a good mindset, good thoughts, good habits, good choices, good behaviors, good mentality, good approach—then an amazing thing happens. What happens is, it becomes so much easier to get *the player* to be where he or she needs to be in their playing of the game, or in their skill development, or in whatever endeavor they are pursuing.

One of the expectations I have set for myself is that I will learn something new every day and that I will, in some way, grow a little bit more every day in my leadership ability. One of the greatest lessons about coaching that I have learned is that, more than anything else, it is about *mentoring*. Which means, being a coach is about relationship. It is about loving the people you are leading; truly caring about their well-being; truly caring about who they are whenever they are not on the field with you; truly caring about who they are going to be in ten years.

So, what does this look like at the pragmatic, day-to-day level? If a player is in a good place as a person, then he is going to be in a good place as a player and as a teammate.

If she is making good and wise choices in other areas of life, then she is more likely to make good and wise choices on the field and court.

If he is handling adversity and difficult situations in life with confidence, toughness and wisdom, then he is more likely to handle adversity and difficult situations on the field or court with confidence, toughness and wisdom.

If she is standing up for the "least among us" in the school hallways and cafeteria and playground, then she is likely going to be a great teammate and leader of the younger, weaker players on the field and court.

If he is working hard to be the best he can be in his classes, in his job, and in his family life, then he is more likely going to work hard to be the best he can be on the field and court.

If she looks for ways to help people and inspire others throughout the normal day, then she is more likely to help make her teammates better and inspire people on the field and court.

If he picks up garbage that he didn't drop or cleans up messes he didn't create throughout the normal day, then he is going to be the first to grab a rake or broom and the first to pick up the dugout or locker room after practices and games.

If time is important to her and she is prompt throughout the day, then time is going to be important and she will be prompt at the field and court.

If being a good person in general and striving every day to be the best he can be is important to him, then you can be sure that value will translate to the field and court.

Get the picture?

Here is the thing, though. The flip side isn't always true. Just because a player works hard at the sport, doesn't always mean he is going to work hard in other areas of life.

That is why we focus on the *person* FIRST, and the *player* SECOND. Who you truly are in life will eventually show itself on the field and court. You can fake it for a while, but your true character will always rise to the top and show itself.

So, if we want to see long-term, deep and unending success in a player, then we need to reach beyond the surface level of just coaching skills in a game. We need to find ways to help mold and shape the player's heart. In the book of Proverbs in the Bible, chapter 4, verse 23 it says, "Above all else, guard your heart, for everything you do flows from it."

I trust in the wisdom of those words, and I have found that it is so much easier to coach players in the skills of the game when the rest of their life is in a good place. Additionally, the opposite (negative side) of this is also true. You can always tell whenever a kid is struggling in life—making poor friend choices, making bad decisions, developing bad habits—by the way they perform on the field or court. Those life experiences always carry over to the athletic field or court and they have a negative impact on both the player as well as the team dynamic.

Finally, I want to say this. My reason for sharing this with you is not just to help you build the best team you can have on the field or court. But I share it with you because I believe our ultimate mission as coaches is to help our players to be the best *person* they can be in all of life. This world needs good people, driven people who love life and are motivated to make it be the best it can be. That's the center of the mark!

Sports, competition, games—these things are all on the fringes of life, but they can all be positively influenced by the ripple effects when we hit the center of the mark. Aim for the *center of the mark* in your coaching. In doing so, you will be most fulfilled and your players will be most successful.

4

A CULTURE OF MISTAKE AVOIDANCE

I am a believer that coaches define the culture. Leaders must define the culture, and then our culture drives our expectations and beliefs. Our expectations and beliefs will then drive our behavior, *how we perform*. So, how a player performs is directly related to the culture you set.

I wonder how many of us have ever said the phrase, "Don't play to *not make a mistake*. Play to win!"

What does that phrase mean, and why do we say it? We say it because we know what happens when teams and players begin playing to *not make mistakes*. There is a different mentality that drives their performance whenever they are playing to not make a mistake. What actually happens is, their minds become focused on mistakes, and then what happens? They make mistakes!

Some coaches not only say the phrase during certain times of a game, some coaches have actually created and developed a culture of *mistake avoidance*. How does that happen? How does it begin? And what is the solution to a changing a culture of mistake avoidance?

Coaches (and parents), let's take a little survey. Answer the following five questions with a simple "yes" or "no." Some of the questions are sport-specific but of course they can be adapted and are relevant to any sport or endeavor:

1. When your player makes an error, are you quick to correct him (coach him up) immediately after the error is made, while he is still on the field or court?

2. Have you ever said these or similar words to your player, "Don't walk this batter," or "You have to make your free throws," or "Do not fumble the ball!"

3. Do you react outwardly—with words, grunts, moans, or other physical gestures—which outwardly communicate your displeasure whenever a big mistake or error is made?

4. Do you feel a need to give verbal coaching advice while your players are in the heat of the game (in the batter's box, on the free throw line, etc.)?

5. Do many of your players react negatively whenever they make a mistake (put their head down, or perhaps even worse behavior such as slam or throw equipment)?

If you answered "yes" to two or more of those five questions, then you have likely created some level of mistake avoidance culture. If you answered "yes" to all five, then there is no doubt that your team is functioning with a mistake avoidance mindset.

I will admit, I was the epitome of all five of those questions for a long time during my coaching career. Even still, I have moments when I will slip up and allow one or two of those kinds of behaviors to be present on my team. It is a very tough discipline for us to maintain a culture that is actually okay with players taking risks and making mistakes. We need to embrace this and realize it can be very good for our teams, as long as there is not only a culture of taking risks but also a culture of learning from mistakes.

That is the key to embracing mistakes—*learning*. You see, the solution to mistake avoidance culture is *not* to be happy about mistakes. We certainly don't *want* to make mistakes, but we just have to help players realize that mistakes cannot be totally avoided. They are going to happen, and sometimes they will happen in big moments. When they do, how will we handle them?

One thing is for certain, you can't change the event that *just took place*—the mistake. No matter how much yelling you do, or how many times you point it out and remind them of it, there is no going back in time to change it. So, the most important thing in that present moment is your reaction, or your response, to the mistake. Your response is going to be the determining factor in the *true outcome* from the mistake.

Too many players, coaches and parents just allow the mistake that happened to consume them, without pausing to consider all the ways that mistake can be used for their *good*.

In the spring of 2017 the high school baseball team I was coaching lost just four games all season. After our second loss of the season, I stood with our team in the outfield for our postgame meeting and said that I refused to look at the game in the traditional terms of "winning and losing," but rather, "winning and *learning*. So, what have we learned today?" We went around and let the players answer the question, and it was a very refreshing time of being able to embrace the loss and learn from it, rather than sulk and bemoan over it and not be able to gain anything from it.

That is the key to mistakes. Learn. Also, consider this: the more mistakes they make, the more opportunities to learn.

Now, I must add this important point. It is much better to make room for mistakes to be made in practice, that way they are minimized in games. Celebrate mistakes in practice, especially when the player made the mistake by being aggressive and taking a risk.

Let players try new things. For example, baseball coaches should let players be their own base coach while running the bases, as long as the ball is in front of them and they can see it. Let them make their own decisions about advancing a base. Is it risky? Sure, but in the long run they will be a more instinctive player and that instinct will put your team in more positions to win than not.

Mistake avoidance causes players to settle for only doing the things they know they *can* do, which means they will rarely ever challenge themselves to do something they *cannot yet* do. Think about that for a second. We want them to grow and reach new levels of skill in the game, but the only way they will be able to do that is if they try new things. Unfortunately, they won't try new things if they are afraid of making a mistake. The result is, they will not grow as an athlete. They will remain in the comfort zone. Nothing great ever happens in the comfort zone. So, embrace the discomfort. You don't have to like it, but embracing it guarantees growth.

Tell your kids, "It is okay to make mistakes when you are being assertive or trying something new." I would much rather have to pull the reins on a kid for being too assertive than to try to get a passive kid to start being assertive. The former is much easier to coach than the latter.

I once read about how in Japanese culture, especially in schools, students at the end of the day are encouraged to look at what worked and what didn't work, and then see how those things could be corrected—thinking of everything as a process rather than looking at results alone.[3]

That is the perspective we need to maintain—process > results. Mistakes are like the blackboards of a classroom. Use them to educate and build young risk-takers into great players. More importantly, you will build mature young men and women who will, as a result, gain one of the great secrets to a lifetime of success.

5

INSTEAD OF THIS, SAY THIS

Words put pictures in our mind. Those pictures will then influence how we feel. How we feel then influences how we perform. It all begins with your words.

A simple thing that I have found to be quite transformational in players and teams is the difference it creates by using *positive* words versus using *negative* words. Another important thing to consider is that some of us may feel like we are being positive and helpful when we are actually being negative and in doing so, we are creating doubt in our players' minds. Of course, we do this unknowingly. I doubt it is anyone's intention to create negative thoughts in our players' minds.

Jon Gordon wrote a really great book titled, "The Positive Dog," which I read one spring during baseball season. Immediately after I read that simple yet profound little fable, I shared it with my team. The idea behind The Positive Dog is: "we all have two dogs inside of us. One dog is positive, happy, optimistic, and hopeful. The other dog is negative, mad, sad, pessimistic, and fearful. These two dogs often fight inside us, but guess who wins the fight? The one you feed the most."[4]

Think about it. Which dog gets fed inside your kids throughout the course of the game? One practical way to make sure the *positive* dog is being fed is to understand the difference between positive words and negative words during the course of a game. There are some words that we may think are positive, but they actually create negative visuals. For example:

"Don't walk this batter."

"Don't swing at bad pitches."

"Don't take a called third strike."

"Don't miss your layups and free throws."

"Don't let that receiver get behind you."

"Don't think too much, just have fun."

Some of those phrases sound like good, positive advice. But the problem is, there is a "negative word" in each of these phrases. The negative word is often the first word or near the beginning of the phrase, and thus the negative word always sets the tone for the remainder of the statement. So, what was intended to be an encouragement actually becomes quite detrimental to performance. How so? Psychologically, this is what happens. Whenever a player hears a word with a negative meaning such as "don't," their brain stops thinking positively and actually focuses on doing something wrong.

The game of baseball, for example, is a very visual game. There is time to visualize, and actually, visualization is good. Skip Bertman, the legendary coach from LSU said, "Everything happens twice. First in your mind, then in reality."[5] What we think about is often what comes to fruition on the baseball diamond. Not always, but very often. The more you visualize something, the better chance you have of it coming to fruition. The best of the best use visualization to their advantage:

- Muhammad Ali always stressed the importance of seeing himself victorious long before the actual fight.

- When Jim Carey was a struggling young actor, he used to visualize himself being the greatest actor in the world before a performance.
- Michael Jordan always took the last shot in his mind before he ever took one in real life.

Many of the world's top performers have mastered the skill of using positive visualization to achieve success. Something that is less documented but just as true, however, is the antithesis of positive visualization. How many times have people failed because of negative pictures that were being played in their minds? They told themselves *not* to do something, but by phrasing it in negative terms, all they could think about was the negative action.

What do I mean by this? Research has suggested that including negative words, such as "not" or "don't" in a sentence can throw off our brains and make it more difficult to understand. Since we think in pictures and tend to visualize the coaching advice that is being provided to us, this can mean that we are actually visualizing what we do *not* want to take place. So, we have to imagine that the human brain has no way of processing the negative-meaning words, which in our previous examples would be the word "don't." If this is true about our brains, then consider what is actually being visualized:

"Walk this batter."

"Swing at bad pitches."

"Take a called third strike."

"Miss your layups and free throws."

"Let that receiver get behind you."

"Think too much."

The thoughts and images we are creating in our players' minds is the opposite of what we intend to create. This happens when we have become so used to phrasing things with *negative* words. Putting a negative thought in the player's mind, even if it is meant to be a positive, causes him to think about the bad result rather than the result you are hoping to achieve. For example, a coach telling his player, "Don't think too much, just have fun," is simply trying to remind the player to relax and just focus on one play at a time and enjoy it. But by beginning the advice with "Don't think too much," it may actually cause the player to think more and to become even more consumed in his thoughts. You know what you are *trying* to say. You just want the player to be athletic and use his instinct, to read the situation and react based on his preparation and skill. So, what if we phrase our advice more like this:

"Ready to react right here!"

"Laying out on this ground ball in the hole!"

"Put this free throw up and in!"

"Stay behind the receiver, keep him in front of you!"

It is a very subtle and simple change in the way we phrase our words, but it has the power to reap very big and significant rewards in the way our teams perform. It is just another example of how positivity always outperforms negativity.

6

YOUR OPPONENT IS NOT THE OFFICIAL

In the early days of my coaching career I had this weird idea that in every game, we were playing against two opponents: the other team and the officials. I am not sure why I viewed things that way, but I did. I went into every game with a chip on my shoulder that at some point during the game we were going to get screwed by the officials. I was always ready for it, and I was always prepared for an argument. As a baseball coach, arguing with officials was "part of the game," I thought.

What a dumb idea.

I made comments about the strike zone. I shouted my disagreement from across the field about every close play that occurred. I belittled umpires and showed them up. And what did it ever gain my team?

I cannot recall one single instance over the years where behaving so negatively toward umpires ever benefited our team in any way. So, why did I do it? Ego, perhaps. Or for some kind of subliminal act of communication that I am "standing up for my team" or defending my players? When it comes right down to it, there is rarely ever a good reason for this kind of behavior.

During any game at any level, of course there will always be decisions that are made by the officials that cause question, or perhaps there will be some legitimately poor judgment calls. When that happens, I have learned that there is a much better way to handle these kinds of things.

It begins with recognizing that umpires and officials are human beings and not machines that are programmed to get everything right, which means they will all be a little inconsistent at times. It also means that they are capable of relationship, and *my relationship* with them is either going to be a positive one or a negative one. We are going to have a relationship, that is unavoidable, because we are in the same event, focused on the same object, and we are interacting during the course of the 2-hour event. So, how I want that relationship to be—positive or negative—is (mostly) within my control.

For this reason, I will always introduce myself before the game, giving my first and last name, and then I will encourage the officials to feel free to refer to me as "Chris" during the game whenever they need anything from me. Likewise, they will typically introduce themselves with their names, and I will ask if they mind if I call them by their first name during the course of the game. To call someone by name is an added level of respect. It feels better, and it sounds better than calling someone "Blue" for example (and most baseball and softball umpires I have met prefer to not be called "Blue"). The point is, when you refer to someone by name it adds a level of humanity and civility, which is definitely needed in our current culture of youth athletics.

The next thing I need to do is be prepared and have a plan. In my mind, I have to already determine that at some point during the game there will be a bad call—maybe even a *really* bad call. Okay, it happens.

Now I won't be so surprised. The key is, *how will I respond to the bad call?* I need to have a plan.

Here is a list of things I have learned to put to rest. I try my best to no longer do these:

- Question calls by shouting across the field
- Immediately react vehemently by running out to argue (from 0-100 MPH in a second)
- Use sarcasm
- Call officials by impersonal names such as "blue"
- Question or protest every little thing

In the event that I feel a call was wrongly made and I feel compelled to discuss it with the umpire, here is the plan I have tried to follow:

1. Wait for the play to fully end, then ask for time out.
2. Calmly walk or jog out to the umpire who made the call.
3. Address him or her by name, and ask if they could tell me what they saw or how they came to the conclusion they came to.
4. Listen to the explanation (this is the most important piece). Truly listen and even repeat to them what they described by asking, "So you are saying that you saw..."
5. Explain what I saw from my perspective, which is the reason for our disagreement, and ask if there is any value to seeking help from the other official(s).
6. Accept whatever answer they give me. I don't have to like it or agree with it, but have to accept it.
7. Thank them for listening and for giving me the opportunity to address them.

I would be lying if I told you that is exactly how all of my disputes with umpires go. But it is my plan, my goal for all of them, which means I will be less likely to be impulsive and react with one of the tactics in the first list above, which I am trying to put to rest for good.

When it comes down to simplest factor, it is just about treating people with respect. It is about recognizing that no one in this life, and especially in the world of sports, is perfect. No one is *trying* to make mistakes. Even the umpires who are really incompetent at the task are not *trying* to be incompetent. I can't believe that anyone *tries* to do a bad job.

I have told my teams, "the day we become perfect in all that we do and the day I make all decisions perfectly as a coach, that is the day we can begin disrespecting umpires." I can confidently say that day will never come.

Umpires are not an opponent. They are not to be seen as someone we have to do battle against. They want the same thing we do—a fair game. It's just that they are the ones with all the pressure on them to ensure that it *is* indeed played fairly.

I will also add this, just like our kids play better when they are having fun, umpires do a lot better when they are having fun. It is hard to do your job when you are always on the defensive, always having to hear how much people disagree with you, always knowing that at any moment someone is going to confront you.

What is to be gained from treating people poorly? It's just ugly. It's nonsense. It helps no situation to become better, and it benefits no person along the way. I encourage you to create for yourself a plan in how you are going to respond whenever something occurs that you disagree with. Use mine if you'd like.

Officiating is not brain surgery, which means there is not zero margin for error. Some are better than others. Sometimes they have good days and sometimes they have bad days—just like you and your team. Even still, I have a feeling that the performance of all officials will get drastically better once they can do their job freely, without feeling a need to be on the defensive.

7

_____

MOTIVATING PLAYERS TO BE THE BEST THEY ARE CAPABLE OF BEING

I do not think anyone or anything *external* can truly motivate a person to do something that they intrinsically do not want to do, or more specifically, something they do not have a strong connection with or passion for doing.

Motivation comes from within. It is *internal*. That's right. It is my belief (and experience) that you and I cannot motivate anyone. Here is why. Because motivation is directly connected with personal responsibility. Every individual person either believes that they *can* or *cannot* control their own behaviors and actions. The person who believes they *can* will be more in control and they will be a motivated person. The person who believes they *cannot* will feel less in control, they will make more excuses, and they will be less motivated.

Motivation comes from within. It cannot be produced externally. That is why there really is no such thing as a "motivational" speaker. There can be "inspirational" speakers. We can inspire others. We can teach people how to find the motivation within themselves to get done what needs to get done, and we can inspire them with lots of things—speeches, music, videos. But none of that will ever be enough to actually get the job done.

Motivation is not something we can *do* to someone else; it is not something we can *give* to someone else. Motivation is the feeling that is already inside a person, and that feeling compels them to either *do* or *don't do* something—to either take responsibility and action or avoid responsibility and action.

This means that all people are motivated all the time. The million-dollar question for coaches is: *what are they motivated to do?* Then, our challenge becomes creating the conditions for which the team members are inspired and determined to achieve the common goals of the team. What we can do is provide them with the energy, the knowledge, the passion, the inspiration, and the goals that will hopefully challenge them to be motivated in positive ways. And if, for some reason, they weren't motivated before, they will see the need for improvement and take the necessary action to make that positive self-change.

You can set the table but ultimately, they are responsible for eating. That is the best way I can think to illustrate it. Trying to "motivate" someone to do something you know they will enjoy and you know they will benefit from is like knowing you have an awesome meal prepared for others that you know is tasty, nutritious and extremely filling. In order for others to be able to enjoy and partake, they first have to *know* about the meal. But even if they know about it, they may still not have the desire to eat it. So, you go to great lengths to make sure the smell of the meal hits their noses, and you set the table with all the utensils and all the delectable courses of the meal so they can see how delicious it looks. Suddenly, they feel like they are getting hungry. They may not have been hungry before, but now, because you have made this meal look so inviting, they can't wait to dive in and devour it!

That is what it means to motivate someone. You didn't make them do something they didn't want to do. You didn't create a hunger inside of them. You didn't conceive a desire inside of their minds. It was there all along. You just made them keenly aware of it. You stirred it up, and you showed them the possibilities. You made them realize that they *can* indeed participate, and you invited them to come along where the eating is good!

People have so much more inside of them than they even realize. They can control aspects of their life and success more than they even realize. Sometimes they just need someone else to come along and shake them, and wake them up to see that. That someone is us, coaches!

EXTERNAL MOTIVATORS

I began this chapter with a claim that real motivation is intrinsic. It comes from within, and there is little you or I can do to actually motivate another person to do something they are not presently motivated to do. We can inspire them, challenge them, and encourage them. But they will not put forth the kind of "motivated" effort you want from them unless they already have, or create, that motivation deep within themselves.

You might ask, "What about external motivators? Is there any value at all from those things that do tend to motivate us but don't come from within ourselves? Is it possible that external motivators *could* actually help a person to create a deeper, internal motivation?"

Those are all great questions. So, I will make a few observations about those "external" motivating factors, their value for sports and for life in general, and whether or not they can actually help lead us to a greater depth of being more internally motivated.

The first observation I'll make about external motivators is that they are temporary. They are good for moments, but rarely last long-term. How many times have we gone to conferences and heard speaker after speaker present to us the best of what they do. We write everything down and make notes of what we want to immediately implement in our own context or with our own teams. We're pumped! We're motivated! Then we get back home and start trying to implement those new and improved ideas—or we try to live and perform differently, just as we determined we would do while at the conference—only to find ourselves in a few short weeks right back into the same old routines we had always had and doing the same old things with our teams.

What happened? We were so motivated while at the conference. Why didn't it last? Because, if we are honest with ourselves, it was only external. It didn't transfer to the deepest part of who we are, to that place where we determine the kind of person we want to be. Our soul. Our essence of being! That is where we have to go. If we *truly* want to understand motivation, we have to focus on the *person*, not the task.

External motivation is like putting a fresh, new coat of paint on a house that is crumbling under its foundation. Sure, it might look nice for a bit. It feels like we really did something to make a great change. But it is only superficial, and it will not take long before it wears off and the same old problem rears its ugly head.

External motivation is focused on *doing*. Internal motivation is focused on *being*. External motivation says, "This is what I want you to *do*." Internal motivation says, "This is who I know you can *be*."

There is the difference. *Being* vs *doing*. I don't just want you to *do* something—play hard, lift weights, lose weight, gain muscle, get faster, hit harder, throw harder, do better in class, get smarter, love better, make better choices—do this, do that, do this and do that.

I can do everything in my power to try to inspire someone to *do* all of those things. And, they may actually do them for a time. But the key is to inspire them to *change* who they are so they will *be* the kind of person that wants to make all of those things an essential part of their life.

True motivation is connected to making the *big* choices about your life. Asking, what kind of person do I want to be? What kind of coach do I want to be? What kind of player do I want to be? What kind of parent do I want to be?

When I have made up my mind about *who I want to be*—the kind of person I am determined to be—then internal motivation for that purpose is what will drive my daily habits. When I am determined to be the best version of me that I am capable of being, then that changes my routines. I won't need a song or a video to get me fired up for that. Sure, a song might help energize me along the way—but eventually the song ends. Eventually that fired-up feeling burns out. Then what do I look to for motivation to keep me going?

Well, if there are no more external motivators available to give me that "feeling" I need in order to keep going, then I guess I'm done. But, if my motivation is based on the deep, intrinsic desire of *who* I am determined to *be*, then nothing can stop me! It will be my way of life!

How many of us have ever gone on a diet in January because we wanted to lose weight and look better for the beach vacation we are planning to take in July? I will raise my hand, I have done that. So, on those journeys, what is your motivation? For many of us, it is a date on the calendar. Let's say the vacation begins on July 15, so we have six months-worth of motivation. Perhaps, to add a little more external motivation, you post to your mirror or fridge an old picture of yourself

38

from a time when you were fit and thin. A visual "motivator" that says: this is what I used to look like, and I want to look like that again.

So, what happens? We eat certain foods and avoid other foods, based on those motivators. We cut out sugary drinks, desserts and empty snacks, based on those motivators. We start exercising, based on those motivators.

Again, what are the motivators? A vacation date and a photo reminder of what we look like when we are in shape.

While we are on this journey, we feel like we are very motivated. And we are, but it is just external. It is not *internal*. How do I know that? Because, what happens once we reach the vacation date and we finally look somewhat like that old, thinner picture of ourselves? All too often we go back to eating poorly or not as healthy and disciplined as we once were. The exercise routine, which was once very important to us when we were "motivated" to lose weight, all of a sudden is not as important anymore and is being pushed out of our daily habits by other things that have suddenly become more important to us. Why? What happened?

What happened is our external motivations are no longer present and therefore there is nothing driving us to continue. Goals are external motivators. Once we reach the goal, we breathe a sigh of relief. There is a sense of accomplishment, and finality. It is finished. I made it.

So, we either need to continually stack up more and more external motivators, which can be exhausting, and eventually they lose their luster anyway. Or, we need a *deeper* motivation. We need a life change. We need an on-going mission for our lives, which defines who we want to be every day, in every circumstance.

Going back to our example, we need to determine that we are going to be the kind of person that intrinsically believes that exercise is more valuable than TV (or any number of other time-wasting things we could substitute for doing what is best for us). We need to determine that we are going to be the kind of person that is not driven by *wants* and momentary desires, but instead we are driven by what we know we *need* and what will give us the best outcomes consistently, not just one time on the calendar. That kind of motivation changes the way you eat—for all of your life, not just until the summer vacation.

See the difference? External motivation is fine for something you just want to accomplish in the moment. But if you want lasting accomplishment, the motivation needs to be deeper.

External motivation is like a one-hit wonder. Internal motivation is like Quincy Jones. It keeps producing and it keeps getting you better and better, for a lifetime.

You can get a team externally motivated for a game, and they'll produce better than normal results in that game. But a team that is *internally* motivated will give you a championship season.

A team that is externally motivated says, "This is what we are going to *do today*." But a team that is internally motivated says, "This is who we are and this is what kind of team we are going to *be* every day." That kind of motivation not only begins a lot sooner than game day, but it also continues long after those players are gone. It builds a winning culture and creates greater expectations for those who will come along after them. It is such a strong and deeply-rooted motivation, that when adversity hits, they don't budge or panic or lose their confidence. They face it and keep moving forward, barely sidetracked from keeping their eyes on their mission.

Do you want to plant seeds for internal motivation in your team and your players? Begin asking them who they want to *be*. The kind of person they are and how they go about their daily, personal habits will always translate to the playing field in the same way. Who they are every day of their lives is who they will be on the field. Oh, and by the way, the same goes for you, coach. We cannot just magically become something we are not. That is the lie of external motivation. Sure, we can pretend for a while. But eventually, *who we are* will always rise to the surface and show itself.

So, coaches, if we want to be better, we need *life* change. We need to go to the deepest root of *who we are*. When on-going mission and life change is what drives our habits and our routines, those things will last much, much longer.

PART II

THE PLAYER

"Good players inspire themselves; great players inspire others."

—Unknown

8

BUILDING BLOCKS OF GREAT TEAMS

It is with intention that I began the section of the book that focuses on *players* by talking about *teams*. With that in mind, I would like to ask you a very important question:

Which is better? To be great? Or, to be part of something much greater than anything you can achieve by yourself?

Which gives you more joy? To be the best player on a mediocre team? Or, to be just one of the members of a *great* team?

Do you want to know something that I find to be a little odd? There is no greater feeling in the world than when your team wins the big one—the championship. And, the higher the stakes, the greater the feeling. It is a tremendous rush of exhilaration. A feeling that you have been part of something really great, something that will be commemorated by generations of people for years to come.

But here is the odd thing. For the majority of players, most of their pursuits are for individual success, often even at the expense of team success. For example, in game situations the majority of players tend to naturally focus more on individual achievement than on helping the team.

Individual pursuits—particularly in a sport such as baseball, which is where most of my own experience has been—seems so often to outweigh team pursuits. Unfortunately, so much of what happens in sports these days is built around individual accomplishments. It is why things like "Fantasy Football" and "Fantasy Baseball" are so popular today. People today are more interested in what their favorite players are accomplishing than what their favorite team is accomplishing. A lot of people today do not even have a favorite team, but they have a favorite player.

Check yourself to see if this is true of you. After you are finished playing a game, which things have you looked at, thought about, and talked about more? Your individual stats and your individual errors? Or, do you spend more time reflecting on the various ways the team was assisted by your contributions?

To use the game of baseball as an example, I wonder how often players really reflect on things that help the team but may not be quite as sexy, such as: getting on base, hitting a sacrifice fly or laying down a sacrifice bunt; or perhaps doing things like being an active base runner that throws the pitcher off his game a little, which results in your teammate getting a better pitch to hit during his at bat?

These are things that are difficult to measure, and they are things that never show up in ESPN's Top Plays, but they are valuable, intangible and unseen realities that are always occurring among champions. There are so many different ways you can help your team. But unfortunately, many of those do not show up in the stat line, and because so many people make judgments about athletes based on numbers—specifically, *your* individual numbers—then most of our focus during games, unfortunately, becomes directed on *me*. My stats, *my* performance, *my* playing time, *my* errors, *my* mistakes—me, me, my, my.

When someone comes to talk to you after the game, they bring up how many points you scored, how many hits you had, or some other individual achievement you may have had during the game. We are consumed with individual achievement. Thus, we are trained to focus on it. We need a serious re-training!

Oh, to have a team filled with players who *always* and *only* think about the TEAM all the time! What would that look like? To have a team filled with players who *get it*—and what I mean by "get it" is that they not only understand it but they embrace it and believe in it. They are motivated and energized by the reality that there are many possible ways they can help the team succeed and be great, even though many of these ways will never show up in the stat lines. That doesn't matter to them. These kinds of things we are talking about are called *intangibles*—qualities and possessions that cannot be quantified, but contribute to success all the same.

The building blocks of a great team are not just great *players*, but great *teammates*. Yes, there is a significant difference.

A collection of tremendously skilled individual players—especially ones who are mostly concerned about themselves, their playing time, their stats, their performance, their successes and failures—are rarely ever talked about late in the postseason because they are rarely ever playing that long. These teams are the ones that often underachieve. So many teams have looked awesome on paper, at the top of the preseason polls, but then underachieve in the long run, while other teams "get hot" late in the season and make a long postseason run. We see this all the time, in nearly every team sport.

Why do some teams seem to *get hot*? What does it take to peak at the right time? We have all seen it. Maybe we have even been part of a team like this. I have had the pleasure of experiencing this phenomenon first-hand. A team gets hot and you hear people talk about how they are *peaking at the right time*. What causes that to happen? What is the difference maker?

I have a theory. It is not very complex or scientific, I will admit. It is what I call the phenomenon of *being a great teammate*.

Oh, it is a phenomenon alright. It is so rare to see one of these kinds of players anymore that when we do see one, they stand out among the rest. We say things like, "There is something different about that guy," and "I like the way he plays the game," and "he has the *it* factor."

The "it factor" is simply, being a team-first player. When you have an entire group of players who are *team-first* players, who are more concerned about the success of the team than literally anything else, who trust the coach's judgment of their talent and their role on the team but continue to practice and prepare just as hard as they possibly can every day—just to be ready in case their name is called, maybe just for one moment—*those* are the building blocks of a great and successful team. And those are the teams that tend to "get hot" at just the right time.

There is nothing magical about it. It is not a supernatural thing that occurs outside of our control. It is actually very much in our control. It is within the control of every individual player on every team, all the time.

It is always within every player's control to *love* his team more than he loves his own accomplishments. It is always within every player's control to *care* about his team more than he cares about his personal success and failures on the field. It is always within every player's control to constantly be thinking about how he can *serve* his team every minute of every game.

Rarely, though, do we see a *majority* of players on any given team who think this way and act this way. Most teams have one or perhaps even a few that do. A team that has *none* who think and act this way is a miserable experience all the way around. But if you can somehow get *every* player on the team to think with a true *team-first* mindset and act with true *team-first* behavior, then congratulations, you have the building blocks of a truly great team. Don't be surprised if you win a championship or two with that group.

Regardless, I can guarantee this, those players and that team will have more fun and make more lasting memories irrespective of what hardware they collect at the end of the season.

PRACTICAL STEPS

Below are some practice points that will hopefully be transferrable immediately into your dugouts, locker rooms and benches. If you want to be a great teammate and you want to try to develop this kind of culture, then put these elements into practice in your own game and on your own team:

- *Desire to play different roles on the team.* Don't just be "okay" with playing different roles, but *desire* it. Want to do it. When you are called upon to sit the bench one game or to be a "role player," think about all the ways you can help your teammates succeed while you are in a role that obviously isn't your dream role. Embracing the smaller role and excelling in it is the first step in eventually being rewarded with larger roles. There are so many roles to play on a team, and when we get ourselves locked into a one-role mindset, we actually limit ourselves (and our team). Flexibility and learning new things is a virtue in any sport.

- *"Think" the game.* Not just as it relates to you and what you are doing, but always think about the broader picture of the game itself. Always keep in the forefront of your mind the notion that the game is much bigger than you, which means it is so egotistical to assume that your mistake, your error, or your one or two great plays that you made are enough to win or lose the game by itself. Translation: *get over yourself.* For most people, the first step in learning how to think like a team player is to simply *get over yourself* and *think the game.* If all we are doing during a game is thinking about ourselves, our failures and our successes, then we cannot be thinking about the team at the same time. Focus on "self" suppresses focus on team.

- *Trust.* When you are a great teammate you automatically create something in other players, and that thing is trust. It is so much easier to trust a team-first teammate than it is to trust a selfish player who happens to be on your team. All championship teams (I have no actual scientific evidence to support this assertion, but I will still go out on a limb and say *all* championship teams) have this quality among their players. They know that each one of them has the same goals in mind as they do. Which means they are never alone in their pursuit of *wanting to be a great team.* Which means they can all trust one another.

- *Love.* Yes, love. The strongest element to any great team is love. They love the game. They love playing the game. And they love each other. When you truly love the people that you are working with to accomplish a goal, be ready! Great things are going to happen! You can be sure of it. Love is the most powerful resource in the world, and it is no different in the sports world. It is why you see hugs and tears along with huge smiles during so many post-championship game interviews. Because people who love one another just accomplished something awesome together, and a big part of the reason why they were able to accomplish such an awesome thing is because *love*, created *trust*, which creates a *new mindset of how to think* about the game, which creates a *desire to play any role* they are given, which is the makeup of a really great team.

Don Mattingly, former New York Yankee and MLB manager, said this about being a great teammate:

> *Team sports are really difficult things. Sometimes your team wins because of you, sometimes in spite of you and sometimes it's like you're not even there. That's the reality of the team game. At one point in my career, something wonderful happened. I don't know why or how, but I came to understand what "team" meant.*
>
> *It meant that although I didn't get a hit or make a great defensive play, I could impact the team in an incredible and consistent way. I learned I could impact my team by caring first and foremost about the team's success and not my own. I don't mean by rooting for us like a typical fan. Fans are fickle. I mean CARE, really care about the team… about "US."*
>
> *I became less selfish, less lazy, less sensitive to negative comments. When I gave up me, I became more. I became a captain, a leader, a better person and I came to understand that life is a team game. And you know what? I've found most people aren't team players. They don't realize that life is the only game in town. Someone should tell them. It has made all the difference in the world to me.*

9

_____

YOUR BEST TEAMMATES

How do you know who your best teammates are? Here is a test that helps bring them to the surface. Watch how a teammate reacts whenever another player—one who happens to play their same position—succeeds or does something really good in the game. Do they get just as excited for a fellow competitor, who happens to be their teammate, as they would for themselves? Or, do they sit quietly and display body language that looks like they are feeling sorry for themselves?

I have seen both reactions. The player who sulks and feels sorry for himself is not a good teammate. He is a *me*-player. He would rather see his teammate fail in order to give himself a better chance to get into the game, regardless of the consequences for his team. This is not the kind of player that championship teams are made up of, and it is not the kind of person that becomes a champion.

Why is being a good teammate so underrated? What has happened to our culture of sports that has caused individual accomplishment to not only overshadow team accomplishment, but completely obliterate it? Today, if you have a team full of players who genuinely desire the success of their team more than their own personal success, then you have something very special and unique. So unique that it could legitimately be one of the last teams standing at the end of the season. Good teammates are the building blocks of great teams, championship teams. It seems so obvious and simple, yet so hard to accomplish.

It requires humility. It requires a servant's heart. It requires a deep and authentic care for the team. I know, I know. When most people are asked, "Do you care for your team?" They will respond, "Of course I care for my team." But actions speak a whole lot louder than words. Caring for your team means you do everything you can to serve your team. It means you are the first to show up for practice because you want to be sure everything is set up and ready, and you are the last to leave because you want to make sure everything is cleaned up properly. It means you look for other ways to help your team, even if those ways are not as glamourous or may be behind the scenes.

But it goes even deeper than that. Caring for your team means you genuinely love your team more than you love your own success. You love your teammates as much as you love yourself. You get excited when your teammates succeed, even if it means you are less likely to get to play as long as they continue succeeding.

This is not an easy role, but it is a necessary role. No team is exempt. Every team needs these kinds of roles fulfilled. Sometimes it might need to be you. When that day comes, will you be ready? What kind of teammate are you?

I had a young man on one of my baseball teams who embodied this role beautifully. He was a junior, and there was a freshman who played his same position who ended up winning the starting position that season. Of course, this meant that the older player would be limited in his playing time. Internally, he had a choice to make. He could feel sorry for himself and quit the team. He could make life miserable for everyone within earshot by complaining that he should be playing instead of the younger player.

There were undoubtedly many negative responses that he could have chosen. Instead, he chose the humble, mature, and I will even call it courageous, response. This kind of team-first behavior takes courage. You cannot be insecure. You have to be strong and confident in who you are. That is what this young man was. He chose behavior that exemplified a true champion.

Once he accepted the fact that his role was going to be different than he had hoped it would be, he actively began looking for other ways in which he could be of service to his team and help his team be as successful as possible. He worked as hard as he could in practice, which challenged other players to also work as hard as they could. During games, he took pride in keeping detailed scouting charts of the opposing teams tendencies and weaknesses. He studied the opposing coach's signs and signals and prided himself in being able to figure them out and steal them.

When one of his teammates succeeded, he was the first to congratulate him. If a coach needed anything, he was the first to volunteer. His team was his first priority. There is something very exciting about that kind of player. They are uncommon and rare to find. This kind of player rarely gets much support, which is why it takes a strong and courageous person to be this kind of player. Often, this kind of player has to explain to his parents that he is okay with his role on the team because his main goal is for the team to be as successful as possible. That means, if the team is more successful while I am in a lesser-playing role, then I accept that and I will do everything I can to love, care for and support my team.

Most of us will find ourselves in this kind of role at some point in our lives. Rarely will anyone *always* be on top of the world and in the exact role where he or she wants to be. At some point we will find ourselves in a "supporting" type of role. The best thing you can be for your team is a great teammate. Even more important than your performance, your production, and your stats is your love for, service for, and care for your team. This is always something you can excel in, regardless of your role.

10

———————

GOALS AND HABITS

"You SAY that you want to _____ (your goal), but the work that you're willing to put in is not going to get you to _____ (your goal). Right now, you have habits that will never allow you to get to _____ (your goal). So, you either have to change the GOAL or you have to change the HABITS."
-Mike Rooney[6]

The message in that statement is very clear. As a coach, it says to me, if I am not daily pursuing opportunities to get better in my communication, in my planning skills, in my understanding of the game, in my own personal habits and work ethic, then I am not going to be able to impart the best possible coaching into my team and players. The message is just as relevant for players, especially those who aspire to be leaders. An old friend of mine once told me, "You cannot lead someone to where you have not yet been yourself." It is simply impossible. You can point and say "Go there," but that's not leadership. That is just giving directions.

Leadership is about "going first" and bringing people with you. If we demand from our teammates things like *positive energy*, but we are always pointing out and thinking about the negative things that have happened and we go through practices with low energy and no fun, then we can't be surprised if that becomes the makeup and culture of our team. If we demand that everyone be focused 100% on practice tasks and getting better during the 2-hour window of time they are at practice, yet we spend the first 20 minutes of practice time socializing instead of being fully engaged in the practice, then we can't be surprised when our team lacks focus and we are not the best we are capable of being on game days.

The very clear message for every player and young person is this: Your *goals* and your *habits* are absolutely and directly related and linked together. If you say that you want to be the best player at your position that your team's program has ever seen, then your habits should reflect that you are putting in the kind of work that is required to become the best at your position, and that you are enlisting the help of coaches and others to provide feedback and knowledge on how to become the best at your position. If your goal is to play college ball, then there are some habits that need to be created that will help you to get to that goal. Additionally, there may be some habits in your life that need to be eliminated because they are going to be counterproductive in helping you reach that goal.

You either have to change the habits, or you have to change the goal.

Every goal in life comes with a certain set of habits attached to it, and the harsh reality is that if we are not—beginning months and years beforehand—engaged in the kind of work and habits that our goals require, then we simply are not going to reach those goals.

The message for every single one of us is this: True leadership is about being able to communicate that truth and then help others to make those changes.

Everyone has goals. Pause for a moment today and reflect on what yours are. Write them down. Goals are based in the future, which means we are not there yet. So, the most important step is to *reverse engineer*, or plan backwards everything it will require from you in order to be able to reach those goals. This is an incremental list of steps of growth you expect you will need to make between today and the date of planned accomplishment.

Then, make another list. This will be your most important list, because it will include some of the habits and behaviors and work ethic that would naturally be required of you if you are going to make those goals become more than just words on a piece of paper.

Too many people in this world, and especially in the world of sports, *talk* about their goals and ambitions more than they actually *work* toward their goals and ambitions. They spend more time posting pictures and quotes and memes about "the grind" on their social media than they actually do participating in *the grind*.

Sit down sometime with your teammates. Be very real with one another. Discuss whether or not you are interested in being the best team you can possibly be. Ask yourselves, do we really *want* to compete for a championship. If we *say* that we do, we have to first make sure we really, truly mean what we say. Because if we really mean what we say, then there will be some regular habits, fundamentals, reps and sacrifices that will be required of every single one of us, every single day, if we are going to be able to reach that goal.

Teams that are great don't happen by accident. They are great because they put in the kind of work that is required according to whatever their goals are. This sounds like a simple concept, but I am continually surprised by the number of people who fail to make this connection. Goals and habits are inextricably related. If you fail to choose to put in the kind of work that your goals require, then you have to change your goals. I don't know who it is attributed to, but there is a popular quote that says, "You do not decide your future. You decide your daily habits, and your daily habits decide your future." This is 100% truth! Your daily habits have to match what you want or else you will never have what you desire.

USING TIME

Talking about creating appropriate habits that line up with our goals would not be complete without talking about perhaps what is the greatest influence on our habits: *time*. Specifically, making the most of *time*, being wiser in our use of *time*, and being a really good manager of *time*.

Time is a common issue among every human. The greatest in any sport are those who can take a 2-hour block of practice time and use it to its fullest extent, getting the absolute most out of all 120 minutes. One of my pet peeves as a coach is wasted practice time. Whenever I see a team practicing and a handful of players are standing around and disengaged for 10 or 15 minutes, I just want to pull them aside and say, "What can you be doing right now to get better, or to help your teammates, or to get in some "mental reps" through visualization?"

There is absolutely no room for any wasted time in any practice, ever. Teams that desire to compete at the highest level and accomplish more than expected are teams that *use time better*. Players who compete at their highest potential and accomplish their goals are the players who have mastered the discipline of *using time better*. It is a discipline, because it is a choice. And because it is a choice, it is completely within our control.

How well do we *use time*? If we are casual with our own time, then it is naturally going to overflow into how we plan (or lack planning) and how we train. If we are too casual with time, we will sacrifice opportunities to grow and get better when we could have just as easily sacrificed a little bit of leisure activity for the sake of our growth and getting better.

Let me suggest something regarding how our personal lives directly affect our teams. I am firm believer that how you are with your team is a mere reflection and overflow of how you behave in your entire life. Do you waste time in your daily life? If so, you will probably find ways to waste time in practices. Are you casual about how you use time? If so, then you will probably be casual about how you perceive and go about time with your team. Does time seem to get away from you? Does it seem like it moves too fast in your daily life, to the point of feeling out of control or like there is just not enough time to get everything done? If so, then it will probably feel the same in relation to your team and practices.

So, let's deal with our *daily lives* first. How do you use time? I realize that is sort of an unusual way to state it, and it is certainly an interesting way to think about it: how do you *use* time? We too often talk in terms of "making time" for something, or "wishing we could make time" for certain things. Those are inaccurate ideas. No one "makes" time. Nobody in the history of the world has ever been able to make or *create* time. Everyone has the same amount of time in a day. Successful people have 24 hours in a day, and unsuccessful people have 24 hours in a day. The *difference* between the two is the management of that time—how they *use* the time.

Reaching your goals begins with creating better habits, and creating better habits begins with using time more wisely. When we get better at using time, then we will develop habits that more accurately line up with our goals.

11

WORK ETHIC OR WANT ETHIC

Everybody wants something. We all have wants. What do you want? What do you want to be? What do you want your team to look like? What kind of player do you want to be? What kind of person do you want to be? What kind of employee do you want to be? What kind of father or mother do you want to be? What kind of husband or wife do you want to be? For our entire lives, we will have wants and wishes and desires for ourselves. And that is good. There is nothing wrong with that.

When it comes to sports, I have heard players and coaches include lots of different things after the words "I want." Most of us want to be better than we are. We want to be stronger, smarter, more athletic, more talented. We want more playing time. We want more opportunities. We want more wins.

We all have wants, and that is fine. However, simply *wanting* something is not what gets the results. I have often heard Tim Kight of *Focus 3* ask the question, "What does the life you want *require* of you?"[7] What his question implies is, if you want something badly, then your want and desire ought to energize you to *do the work* that is required to produce your want—to turn your "want" into reality.

Too often, however, too many people only get as far as having the *want*. Too many people have the *want* but not the *work*. Without the work, all you will end up with is a lifetime of wanting, or eventually wondering "what could have been."

Have you ever attended a workshop? A workshop is built around the idea of bringing a group of people to a common place and then presenting helpful information and strategies that everyone can then take back home and implement with their own team, business, or school. Workshops are, by nature and namesake, meant to send us home with things to "work" on, and as a result of our work, we get better.

I have attended many workshops in my lifetime, but I have never met anyone who has ever attended a *wantshop*. I suppose a "wantshop" would be a seminar where we gather a bunch of people into a room, and then everyone thinks really hard about all the great things they would like to have happen in their lives or with their teams or their businesses. And that is all. It ends there. That is as far as it goes.

Do you think there could be a market in the world today for "wantshops?" We could bring together teams of coaches and players and have them all think really hard about what they want the team to perform like and accomplish this season. Then we will send them out and wish them luck!

That sure sounds like an absurd idea, but it is more actual than you might realize. So many people *want* to be great, but the work they actually put in does not match their desire. So many people talk about what they are planning to accomplish, but their life and their actions and their behaviors and their daily habits do not align with their words and their wants.

I have heard kids (and coaches) talk about how they really *want* to see their team succeed this season, and they talk about all the potential they have. But if you asked them what they are doing right now, in the off-season, to actualize that "want," many of the answers simply do not align with what it takes to bring their *want* into existence. They are not going to reach the potential they believe they have, and their want will always be just that—a *want*—because they are not doing the *work* that is required to create what they want to accomplish.

Why does this happen more often than not? Why do we fail to do the work required to get the things we want? Here is what I think. I think too many people don't like the inconvenience that being great causes. We prefer easy over challenging. We don't appreciate the long-term. We hate having to wait for anything and want everything to happen instantly. We too easily give in to spontaneous whims based on what we *feel* like doing in the moment, rather than having a disciplined plan and sticking to it. We have become accustomed to getting just enough to satisfy us without having to inconvenience ourselves with extra work.

Too many of us prefer easier, faster rewards that require less discipline and less work. And guess what? These are not new issues. We are not living in some special time today and dealing with things that the world has never before seen. We are essentially dealing with the same things that anyone who has ever wanted to be great has had to deal with. We are just dealing with it in our time and in our context.

You will not hear me say things like, "Oh, kids these days. They are so lazy. They want everything handed to them. They lay around playing video games for hours and hours and then wonder why they aren't getting any better at their sport."

Laziness and unrealized potential are not new phenomena. These things have been around for generations. That does not mean we should excuse it or give in to it, but we just should not be surprised by it. Instead, acknowledge the fact that it is normal. It is actually what comes most natural in the majority of teenagers. The good news is, no one has to accept it as the only way to live. We all have the choice to live a more excellent life and model a more excellent way.

There is always *work* that is required to achieve the things we *want*. It is up to each one of us to make sure our life's *wants* and our life's *work* are aligned. When a lifetime of that pattern materializes over and over again, that is the process of building the champion within yourself!

12

ELITE

There has been a trend in recent years among club sports teams to add the word "Elite" to the identity of their team. A question this brings to my mind is, are all these teams truly living up to their name?

What does *elite* mean? Are these teams and players truly elite, or is it just a word that has been casually thrown into the team name to make it sound good or to try to communicate the level of player they *hope* to be able to attract to the club?

Words matter. Using a term like "elite" to identify a group of people or a team has become fashionable, but it causes me to pause and contemplate what it means to truly be elite, and are all these teams and players who are wearing the name "elite" actually accomplishing that endeavor?

The Merriam-Webster Dictionary defines "elite" in these ways: (noun)

- the choice or best of anything considered collectively
- persons of the highest class

- a group of persons exercising the major share of authority or influence within a larger group

(adjective)

- representing the most choice or select; best

To make this personal, let's think of elite in terms of you and more specifically, your everyday behavior. What does *elite* look like, every day? What distinguishes you as a person from being *average* to being *elite* in your daily behaviors? In athletics, academics, and all of life, there is average and there is exceptional (there is also below-average, but I doubt that anyone who falls into the below-average category is reading this book). How can we know whether or not we are just cruising along in life with autopilot behaviors that make a person average, or if we are being intentional about "representing the most choice or select" version of all that we are, or if we are being *the best* of who we are?

That is a great definition of elite. Many coaches and leadership development professionals define elite like this: *being the best version of you.*

Do you know what the best version of you looks like? I can tell you this, it will *not* be found by comparing yourself to anyone else. We may not actually know right now what the best version of *me* looks like, but we *can* learn how to get on the *road* to elite. Yes, elite is a journey, a process. It is something you can *become*. It is not something you inherently are. Elite is not just naturally ingrained in a person. You must journey to elite.

The road to elite and journeying every day on that road, looks like this: *be better today than you were yesterday, and be better tomorrow than you are today.* Just a little bit. Just 1% better each day, if it helps to think in incremental terms.

This is incredibly motivating to me. To know that I have what it takes within myself to be elite, because elite is defined as *my best*. Not *the best*, which is in comparison to others, but the *best version of me* that I am capable of being. This way of thinking about being elite is incredibly motivating.

Here is why it is motivating. If we don't actually know what the best version of ourselves looks like, then that means we are capable of achieving things that we are not even aware of yet. It means there are accomplishments and successes in our future that we would never have imagined we are capable of achieving. But those will only come if we take the *road* to elite; if we choose our behaviors and our words and our responses to circumstances with discipline rather than with knee-jerk, impulsive reactions. Or, rather than because it is the easy choice, or the common choice, or the choice that feels good at the moment, or the choice that the majority of the crowd is going with.

The majority of the crowd in this world is *not* on the road to elite. The majority of the crowd in this world—in any given team or organization—is just fine with the comfort of the highway to average. In school, there are lots of students who *could* do a lot better, but they are okay with average. They literally do not *have* to stay in the realm of average. They may never finish at the top of their class, but they most certainly could work at a more elite level for themselves. Yet, they choose the easy road.

There is comfort in average. There is comfort in being in the middle. It is where most people live, and so it is easy to just settle in and assume that is where we belong too. Mediocrity. Basically, just place life on cruise control and do what you know you *can* do, what you are used to, rather than seeking to do what you don't even realize you are capable of doing. It takes courage to step up and choose the road to elite. But the more you do—in small ways, becoming 1% better every day—the easier it gets, because you are building new habits. The kinds of habits that only the *elite* are characterized by.

No one *belongs* in mediocrity. No one *belongs* in average. It is where most people end up, unfortunately. But it is not where you belong. Get that out of your head right now. You *can* get onto the road to elite. If you want your team to truly be elite, not just in name but in action and behavior, it *can* be. It will not be, however, if you are not taking steps on the road yourself. That is why the focus of this chapter has been on you, personally. Because something all elite teams, organizations, or groups share is that their leaders and their people are elite in their behaviors, choices, and attitudes.

The good news for all of us is that there *is* a way for all of us to be elite, and it is not just by putting the name on your jersey. Sure, "Southeast Prospects Elite" might sound catchy as a team name, but is your team doing what it takes every day to be the best version of themselves that they are capable of becoming? Are your players doing what it takes every day to be the best versions of themselves that they are capable of becoming? Are the coaches doing everything they can to be the best version of themselves that they are capable of becoming?

If not, then please take the word "elite" off your jersey.

If you are not sure whether or not this describes you or your team but you truly want to be on the road to elite, here is a brief word about how to begin. It starts with checking your mindset. The one thing you can *always* choose, whether you believe it or not, is your mindset.

While the *average* mind says, "My life is too busy to make sure I am getting plenty of sleep in order to function at my very best every day." The *elite* mind says, "Yes, I may be busy but it is possible, and here is how I am going to arrange my time in order to make it happen."

While the *average* mind says it is easier and more fun to consume foods and drinks that have no nutritional value and it is more convenient to eat junk food, the *elite* mind says, "Yes, I know those foods taste delicious and it takes more preparation and discipline to be able to eat healthier, but food and drink isn't just for pleasure. Food and drink is the fuel of the body, and my body is going to benefit or suffer depending on and directly relating to what I am fueling it with. Therefore, I will be more intentional about what I choose to put into my body."

While the *average* mind says I deserve a break and I have earned the right to "veg out" and binge watch Netflix or do something mindless for hours such as video games or TV, the *elite* mind says, "Yes, but I can be so much more useful with my time and still get as much enjoyment out of it by reading, listening to a podcast, exercising, or doing some act of service for someone else (mow a lawn, rake leaves, shovel snow, wash dishes), or practice a skill in something that I want to be elite in."

There is a *reason* why the people who are at the top of their field, their game, their life, are there. It is because they are doing *not* what the average person does in any given scenario, but they are *choosing* the more difficult, uncommon practices of the elite. It is not that they don't know that all those average choices are options, it is just that they prefer to not automatically choose those things that the average person chooses. They choose to change their mindset from the *average* way of thinking to the *elite* way of thinking.

You can do it too! Honestly, most people will not do it. I guess there is a reason why we even have a word like "elite." Because if most people chose the elite road then it would no longer be elite, it would be the common way of life.

I hope you will take encouragement in this and get excited about the possibility that each one of us *does* have what it takes to be elite. We have the choice. Actually, I should say *choices*, because it is not just one choice at one point in time. No one just chooses one day, "I'm going to be elite," and then they are! *Go ahead and screen-print it on a jersey. See, I am elite!* No, sorry, it doesn't work that way. It is not something you decide one day and then you *are*. It is something you *become*, and the "becoming" occurs little by little, every day, as you get better at making those elite choices over the average choices.

How does this relate to teams? What makes teams elite? When athletes take ownership of this and live a life of choosing the elite road over the average road, just watch and see how it begins to translate onto the playing field. You, as an athlete are not just a machine that goes out to a field or court to perform a skill in hopes to win a contest. We are human beings, holistic, which means every aspect of our lives affects the other. When we understand this and *live* it every day, in all aspects of our lives, that is when our teams rise to the level of elite. And, it doesn't matter whether it is printed on our jerseys or not.

13

THE INVISIBLE GAME WITHIN THE GAME

Whenever we watch an athletic contest either live or on TV, what do we see? We see physical movements, physical skills, and sometimes incredibly athletic physical achievements.

What we don't see is the other half of what is actually going on, and the reason why we don't see it is because it is invisible. It is taking place inside the minds of the athletes on the field or court.

Take a survey of your teammates sometime, asking them the question: "By percentage, how much of playing the game of _____ (enter any sport) would you suggest is *mental?*"

I always ask this question of my teams, and I always receive answers varying from 50% to 75% to even as high as 90%. The point of the question is not to get the answer correct. I am not sure anyone really knows what percentage of the game is mental. Yet, we *all* know that at least *some* portion of it is, and it is likely an even greater percentage than we think.

The main point of asking such a question, however, is actually the follow-up question. Let's say we agree that 50% of the game is mental.

In saying that, we are saying that *half* of your success in the sport you are playing is going to be dependent on how well you handle all of the mental aspects of the game—how well you handle failure, adversity, pressure, anxiety, stress, nerves, anger, frustration, errors, mistakes, and even success.

Now, if in fact 50% of the sport you play is mental, then how much time are we devoting in our training and in our practice to prepare in the mental game? What kinds of skills are we working on to help strengthen our responses to difficult and frustrating situations that we know will always occur in every game?

I will admit, I spent several years not even considering this at all. Even after coming to an awareness that the mental game was important, I still didn't know how to apply it and certainly had no means to implement it into practices so that my players could train to get better at the mental game.

It takes a little bit of creativity, but it can be done. I love the way Coach Dave Hilton defines the mental game. On Brian Cain's Peak Performance Podcast, he stated it this way: "When we talk about the mental game, we are talking about the *mental skills* and routines you need in order to be able to take your *physical skills* to their full potential *while under pressure.*"[8]

I love that wording, "mental *skills* and *routines*." Yes, you can practice and build *mental skills*, and the way this is done is by understanding the power of *routines*.

Every successful person in the world knows and understands the power of having and developing routines that feed your mind, body and soul in positive ways. We all have habits, and our habits are either giving us better life and more energy, helping us to succeed and grow and get better in every situation we face. Or, maybe our habits are actually having the opposite effect; they are sucking the life out of us, slowing us down and gradually killing our spirit and our ability to deal with situations effectively.

Before we talk about how to create routines to practice mental skills, let's consider some of the situations that occur in games that players sometimes have a difficult time dealing with. Since my primary context has been baseball, I will list examples from the game of baseball. Here are some that immediately come to my mind:

- striking out

- popping out

- grounding out

- making any kind of out

- making a defensive error

- giving up a home run while pitching

- walking a batter

- umpire making a bad call

- opposing team heckling or getting mouthy toward you or your team

These are some of the most common situations that occur in a baseball or softball game, which require mental toughness and more importantly, mental training and skill in order to be able to deal with them and move on and overcome the adverse situation.

How do we train mentally? How do we build mental skills to be able to deal with such adversity? It is possible to be intentional about working on your mental game. This is how I have done it with players and teams I have trained. The first thing I like to do is ask them a question: "Why are we always so surprised whenever something negative happens in a game?"

Think about that for a second. How often does a baseball player make an out during an at-bat? There is no exact answer, but it is accurate to say "more often than they are safe." Even the greatest players in the world make outs more often than hits. How often does an official make a bad call? How often do errors occur?

All the time, right!? Those things are a regular and consistent part of the game, and if anything is certain, it is that these things *will* happen. So, why do we act like we are always so surprised whenever these things occur?

One reason, perhaps, is that we feel like we are setting ourselves up for failure if we anticipate something negative. We prefer to not put into our minds any thoughts of possible failure. We say things like, "failure is not an option," and we make ourselves think that if we fail it is final and definitive. Seth Godin suggests, "Anyone who says failure is not an option has also ruled out innovation."[9] We learn from failure. We grow from failure. Failure is not the final verdict, ever.

It is possible for you to teach yourself that failure and adversity are to be expected during the game but that doesn't mean you have to take it in stride and be okay with it. You don't have to *like* it. The key is controlling how you *respond* to it.

I think this is why some people react to failure the way they do—with extreme anger, and throwing or slamming pieces of equipment—because they don't want to appear as though they are "okay" with failure. They are competitors, which means they expect to succeed *every* time. There is nothing wrong with having that expectation, but the realist in me says that any reasonable person certainly knows deep down inside that they are not going to bat 1.000, they are not going to throw no-hitters and shutouts every time they pitch and they are not going to go undefeated every season. There *is* going to be failure. It is certain. We have to know that it is coming.

The irony is, this is the first step in not allowing failure or adversity to defeat you. The first step is to be aware that it *will* happen. Once we embrace that acknowledgement, then we ask ourselves this question: "Okay, since I know something bad or frustrating is going to occur at some point, *how am I going to respond to it when it happens?*"

What is your plan? What is your routine going to be for dealing with the frustration, flushing it away from your mind and moving on to the next play?

I have my players write it out. It is part of their homework during the first week of the season. I want them to think about and write out the actual routine they are going to use when they are approaching a "red light" moment.

We call this their "red light" routine, and it is what they will do whenever they recognize that their frustration level is high. Basically, we want to operate our regular lives in the "green light" zone. Likewise, our goal is to play the game in the "green light" zone. When everything is green, everything is going well. When we are in the green zone, we are most focused, most productive, most confident, and most successful. However, sometimes things don't go as well, and we find ourselves getting a little bit upset. Those are "yellow light" moments. When we are in the "yellow" zone, it should trigger us to slow down. Get perspective on things before we get to "red." Our goal, of course, is to be able to recognize when we are getting close to "red" and prevent ourselves from ever getting that frustrated. But sometimes, it is unavoidable. When you see "red," it means STOP. Red light means *press pause.*

So, the first step of our routine, whenever we have just experienced something extremely frustrating, is to *press pause.* Whatever your first instinct is—whatever your impulsive reaction to the situation is—pause it, and choose to not allow that impulse to win.

Second, right after *pressing pause* in your mind, take a deep breath. This is called a *releasing* breath, because it is used to "release" the bad thing that just happened. Breath in for three seconds—a deep, belly breath. Hold it for one second, then exhale. This slows your heart rate down, and it slows everything down in that moment. It also provides a physical process to blow the bad situation out of your mind. It is a "releasing" deep breath.

Third, do something *physical*. Take your hat off and wipe the sweat from your brow, or any number of small, simple, physical acts. This step takes your mind off the bad thing that just occurred and gets you ready to focus on the next pitch.

Finally, the fourth step is to take another deep breath, and this one is taken while your eyes are fixed on a small object, a focal point. This second deep breath is a *refocusing* breath. Taking a deep breath on a particular focal point helps your mind to slow everything down and focus on one thing: *the next play* or next moment.

Now what we have is an actual routine to help us be mentally stronger while playing the game. In the same way that we have fundamentals and drills to help us become better at physical skills, we now have a routine that strengthens our minds and our focus while performing those physical skills of the game. It is a mental strength routine that enables you to take your physical skills to their full potential while under pressure.[10]

Just like throwing bullpens are important for pitchers to be prepared to compete on the mound and taking batting practice and ground balls helps to prepare players to compete against an opponent, in the same way, the mental routines we have are just as important to implement into our training. If we truly believe that as much as 50% of the game is mental, meaning that it requires mental strength in order to be able to succeed, then we should probably devote *at least* 10% or so of our practice to mental reps and building mental skills, wouldn't you agree?

We use a couple different methods in our practice plans to rep our mental routines. During live batting practice, we implement the "red light" routine as one of our stations. We have our pitchers throw "shadow" bullpens (these are basically "pretend" bullpens with no ball or catcher), to imagine various situations that can and will come up in a game, in which they will need to be ready to respond positively. They also practice pre-pitch routines and their "red light" routines in those bullpen sessions.

The mental reps in our practices are taken seriously. We want every player to recognize how valuable it is for them to be able to instinctively respond to frustrating things with their mental strength routine. In the same way that they had learned to instinctively respond to the *physical* aspects of the game through normal practice routines, they now have the tools to be able to practice and grow in the *mental* aspects of the game.

In baseball, I have seen many players with a picture-perfect *swing* but their approach during the at-bat, their mental preparation while waiting to bat, and their responses after missed pitches or bad calls, are all actually quite weak and reveal a lack of preparation, and ultimately a serious hole in their game. They think hitting is only about *swinging the bat*.

I will put it this way, if you go to a hitting instructor and all the coaching you receive is solely on your swing and your mechanics, then you are only getting half your money's worth, because that coach is only teaching you 50% of how to be a great hitter.

You see, that is the magic question. Do you want to have a *great swing?* Or do you want to be a *great hitter?* Being a great hitter involves being mentally prepared, mentally strong, and understanding the importance of your overall "approach."

This same principle is true in all aspects of the game, and it is true for other sports as well as all other aspects of life. You know adversity is coming. Don't be surprised by it. Be prepared. Have a plan.

14

WHAT WE CAN CONTROL

One of the greatest moments of growth for me personally was when I finally began to make the conscious effort to stop talking about and thinking about things that I had no control to change or influence. I had always known this to be a virtuous characteristic that the best coaches, teams and players possessed, yet I had never actually put it into practice myself. I knew that it did no good to allow my mind to dwell on things that were outside of my control, yet I still permitted my thoughts and my words to go to those places regularly. This habit is one of the most seriously hindering behaviors of any athlete, coach or team.

Finally, I said, *enough is enough!* I will no longer be influenced negatively by things that I cannot control. I will no longer allow my mind and my mouth to enter into negativity and frustration because of something that is completely outside of my ability to make any effective change for the better. So, I suppose you can say that the first step was recognizing it was a problem and admitting to myself that I needed to take some very real and practical steps to change this behavior.

The first thing I did was make a list of as many things I could think of that neither I nor anyone else on our team could control. I literally wrote them down. The list included (but is not limited to):

- the weather
- playing conditions
- travel issues
- officials' decisions and poor calls
- opponent's behavior
- where the ball goes after our players swing and hit it
- the kind of play an opponent makes on a ball we hit
- how hard or how slow the opposing pitcher throws
- rules of the game (particularly the ones we think are silly)
- anything that happens in the bleachers or outside of our dugout
- expectations of other people

These are just some of the things that will always try to distract you in pretty much every game you play. Focusing on these things to the extent of allowing them to get a reaction out of you will do nothing but weaken your competitiveness and ultimately weaken your team.

I can remember making a conscious decision and commitment to stop talking about and thinking about these uncontrollable things. Once I had identified what they were by writing them down, I could more easily recognize them whenever my mind was tempted to dwell on them. I would immediately have the option to grab hold of the thought and kill it before it could grow into a verbal comment or outward display of frustration, which would subsequently start bringing others down on my team.

Negative thoughts and reactions to things outside our control are like a deadly virus on a team. Once one person starts focusing on and complaining about something, it then becomes easier for the next person to start focusing on that or another uncontrollable and complain about it, and then the next person, and so on and so forth, right on down the line to every teammate and every coach. This phenomenon absolutely kills team focus. It kills competitiveness.

Why? Because it creates one of the deadliest threats in the universe: *an excuse*. Dwelling on and complaining about something we have no control over is like saying, "I have an excuse for why I can't succeed." The more we do it, the less we succeed. It is that simple.

After I had made myself aware of an actual list of things that I could not control, it made my mind conscious of those things whenever they would rear their ugly head during a game. In those moments, I would then have a choice (a choice is something we *can* control): to think about that thing and complain about it, or to ignore that thing and let it pass.

Ignoring things that you have no control to change does two really amazing things, and these will be an immediate effect:

1. It relieves you of stress, because most stress is caused by worries or frustrations about things we cannot change.
2. It gives you a lot more time to focus your attention on the things that truly matter *most*—the things of which you actually do have control.

I want to be sure to emphasize this. I am not suggesting that the things we can't control don't matter at all. To think that way is disingenuous, like trying to fool ourselves into believing something doesn't matter when we know that on some level it actually does matter.

But the point is this. Whether the uncontrollable matter is really significant or really small, the fact remains that it is *out of your control.* Which means, the fact remains that if you focus any amount of energy worrying about or complaining about that uncontrollable matter, then what you have done is nothing but completely waste your energy, waste your time, waste your words, and waste your influence. Regardless of how much or how little that thing matters or troubles you, dwelling on it and allowing it to get a reaction out of you is a complete *waste* of your resources.

Let's flip this around. How do we respond to uncontrollable things in a positive manner? What *should* we focus on whenever we start to recognize that an "uncontrollable" is fighting for and gaining some of our attention?

The obvious answer is: focus on the things we know we *can* control. What are some of those things?

- *Attitude.* Your mindset, whether positive or negative, is *always* within your control. As much as we try to deny this, it simply is true that we always choose for ourselves how we are going to think about and respond to a certain scenario. We can be influenced positively or negatively by circumstances, but the only person who owns and is responsible for our attitude is ourselves. The sooner we embrace this truth, the sooner we begin to change for the better, and the sooner we stop blaming others, blaming circumstances, and making excuses for our own selfish and childish responses to things that upset us.

- *Effort and work ethic.* No one controls how fast you run, how strong you get, how determined you play, or how you go about your business. The one and only person who decides how fast you are going to run from Point A to Point B is *you.* The one and only person who decides how much preparation you are going to give is *you.* Effort and work ethic is 100% within our own control.

- *Reaction to events.* No one is forcing you to react one way or the other. You have complete and total freedom to react positively, and if you choose to react negatively then remember, that was your choice. No one or nothing *made* you do that.

- *Rest and Diet.* No one is force-feeding you. No one is making you stay up late and not get enough sleep. Even if you have a busy schedule, we all have things that we could eliminate or cut back in order to make room for more rest (i.e. social media, TV, video games, Netflix). Turn off the electronic device for just one hour a day and see how much difference it makes in the amount of time you have. Some of us do not even realize how much time we spend staring at a phone. *You* are the one who is choosing the way your body feels and performs. It is amazing to think that this is something we have control over, yet this is one of the areas we so frequently give up control and then we become frustrated when we don't feel well or perform as well as we wished we would have. We have the power to change that.

- *Preparation.* Our own preparation for the things we care about is always completely within our control. How we prepare, how much time we give to preparation, our focus during the preparation, is all within our own ability and control to determine.

Those are just a handful of things that fit into the "things I control" list. There are so many more things, such as: enthusiasm, aggressiveness, attention and focus, words and language. Sometimes, being able to focus more on the things we can control is linked to our ability to maintain a proper perspective on things. We will discuss this in the next chapter.

15

IT COULD BE WORSE

In the summer of 2010 I was coaching an 11U baseball team. I have many memories of that particular season and team, but one moment stands out among the others. We were playing in our hometown tournament, the *Throw-Down In A-Town,* and we were having a little bit of a rough time in pool play. Several of our players were having bad games and they were starting to get discouraged internally and then they were expressing that discouragement externally. Kids who normally would never slam a glove or helmet or "forcefully place" a bat back in the rack were doing so with regularity, and they were openly verbalizing their disdain for the umpires and their own failures. Unfortunately, our coaches were all experiencing the same frustration and, needless to say, were not handling it much better than the 11-year old kids.

I remember feeling lost about how to handle it. I knew something had to be done before things got even more out of control. It was late Saturday night when I came up with an idea. It wasn't my idea, it was something I remembered hearing Skip Bertman talk about with his

LSU Tigers team in the early 1990s. I thought, "Why not, let's try it!" So, the first thing I needed to do was sit down at my computer to do some research. I looked up a number of recent news articles that told of various tragedies or adversities people have had to endure in their lives. There was an article about a young girl who was recently diagnosed with cancer, another article about a family that was in a fatal car accident, and another article about a young boy who had been confined to a wheelchair all of his life, and he talked about how much he loved baseball yet had never been able to play on a team until a league in West Virginia was developed for individuals with disabilities.

I printed all of those articles out and glued them to a big piece of poster-board. At the top of the poster board, in bold black marker I wrote: *"Did you just strike out? Pop out? Make an error? Make a mistake? Make a bad pitch? It could be worse, a lot worse."*

Underneath those words were the various articles I had printed out and pasted to the poster-board. I got to the field extra early the next morning and taped that big poster-board to the far side of the dugout, above the bench. When all the players and coaches had arrived, I pulled them together before warmup and explained to them that I had been up late the night before, trying to come up with a way to help us all to come into this new day with a better perspective on what we were doing—*playing a game!*

Then I showed them the poster-board hanging at the end of our dugout. I said, "Today we will all have a new procedure. Any time and *every* time something happens during the game that causes us to get angry, frustrated, discouraged, or any other negative emotion, we will be required to walk down to the end of the dugout, read the poster-board, choose one of the articles, and read it for 20 seconds. After reading, take a deep breath, put on a smile (force one if you have to), then run onto the field or move on to your next task."

This exercise was for our coaches as well, and we all needed it just as much as the kids needed it. Coaches sometimes need it *more* than the kids do. We could also include parents; perhaps we should post one of those poster-boards on the *outside* of the dugout as well.

The point is, it was such a crucial thing to be able to pause for a moment, in the heat of the moment, and be reminded of how blessed we were to be able to be out there on a beautiful afternoon, enjoying a game, when things *could be a lot worse.*

16

THE "NOT TWO IN A ROW" RULE

I was sitting in the stands watching my son's college baseball team play. The opposing pitcher had thrown a perfect game through 4 innings in the second game of a double header, in which they were only playing 7 innings per game. This meant he only had 3 more innings to go in order to complete the perfect game. Just 9 outs. You could tell he was feeling it.

In the 3rd and 4th innings he had worked out of a jam, falling behind on a couple batters but then getting them to fly out or ground out. With every new out, he expressed his enthusiasm. Then, in the top of the 5th inning with one out, he walked a batter. As soon as he threw ball four, he took off his hat, slammed it to the side of his leg and blurted out a colorful word as he walked around the mound. Visibly, and audibly, frustrated.

At this point, while the perfect game was no longer in-tact, the no-hitter was obviously still in play. However, I could see that he had not *let it go* by the time he had stepped back onto the pitcher's mound to throw the next pitch. That's when I leaned over to my wife, April, and said these exact words: "Because the pitcher is still thinking about the walk he just gave up, he is going to give up a base hit in this inning too."

The very next pitch to the very next batter: base hit up the middle. Just like that, the "no-no" was no more! One mistake was permitted to become two in a row.

Yes, I say "permitted," because I believe that we have the ability to influence these kinds of things. In sports such as baseball and softball, one error or mistake doesn't devastate you. The key is to flush it and not let it become two in a row. Teams that do this regularly are elite. They know they are going to make mistakes. The difference is, they have just mastered the "not-two-in-a-row rule." And the difference-maker in this is *mental strength*.

Not understanding this truth is where so many coaches and players alike end up compounding the issue. They think the solution is physical. More ground balls, more swings, run until you puke (and somehow that will keep you from making multiple errors and giving up big innings). I have never understood that logic.

The fact is, the secret to being able to overcome the mistake and not allow one mistake to become two, then three, is *not* physical. It is mental. It is knowing how to react when something "bad" happens. First, as I have mentioned in a previous chapter, it is important to not allow yourself to be surprised when something bad happens. Then, you must have a plan for how you are going to respond when something bad happens.

Everyone makes errors. The best in any sport are those who have learned how to not let one mistake become two in a row. Those who cannot let it go usually only end up making things worse. The bad event that just happened does not have to completely define the final outcome. The most important factor in the outcome is your *response* to the bad event. Your response influences the outcome as much as the event itself. This is awesome news, because it means that while we can't control the event, we *can* have some control over the outcome! And the reason this is true is because we can totally and absolutely control our response to the negative event.

How is this done?

The first step, I will reiterate, is learning to not be surprised when bad things happen. Sports are full of adversity. It happens, we know it happens, every game. Yet, some players and coaches get all bent out of shape and act like they were surprised, and just cannot let it go. Of course you are disappointed. You didn't *want* the negative event to happen, and you were not *expecting* it to happen (hopefully you weren't). But, "not being surprised by it" means that you were *prepared* for how you would respond whenever something of that nature does happen. Which means, you are never taken to a place of being *out of control* of your thoughts and actions. Which means, yes, you can for a moment allow yourself to feel the disappointment of the negative play but then immediately know what to do in order to flush it away and refocus all of your attention on the *next* play.

This is the point where *pressing pause* and taking a deep breath occurs, allowing you to blow the bad play out of your mind. Release it!

Then, you need to recognize that your mind is going crazy right now. It is telling you how bad that last play just was, how much it is going to hurt the team's chances, and all sorts of other distracting, non-productive things. Stop *listening to yourself*, the voice inside your head, which is still grumbling to you about the last play. Instead, start *talking to yourself* about what you are going to accomplish on the next play. Visualize the next positive play, verbalize to yourself what you are about to do, and then you are ready to get it done!

Finally, take another deep breath. This time, zero your eyes' focus on something small for that entire three to four seconds of the deep breath. This again slows the moment down, puts everything that just happened in the rearview mirror and gets you 100% focused on the present moment, ready for the next play.

This routine will probably need to be done a dozen times per game, or more. Think about it. In any given game, how many ground balls or fly balls are hit in your direction? Maybe three or four, on average. How many pitches do you swing at in a typical game? Maybe four or five, give or take. But, in any given game, how often does something adverse occur which you need to be prepared to handle in a positive and constructive way?

Now, here is a very important follow-up question: how often do we *practice* that part of our game?

You can practice 100 more ground balls a day and take 100 more swings a day, and none of that will help you with this, perhaps most important aspect of the game. You have to practice the mental game. You have to train and prepare yourself mentally in the same way you train and prepare physically. Have a plan. This is so important that I have made a point to mention it multiple times in this book. Practice that routine during your training and during your team's practice times. Practice it in all of life, whenever something adverse comes your way. It will not only make you a better player, it will make you a better person. A better student. A better son. A better daughter. A better husband. A better wife. A better employee. A better leader.

Tyler Tervooren hosts a blog that assists and trains leaders in developing qualities for success. In one of the articles he discussed a simple principle of success that all great leaders have learned to master: *don't fail twice in a row*. Here is an insightful quote from the article. The context is developing good habits:

I don't claim to have all the answers, but I think this is a big part of what accounts for success: never failing twice in a row. If you compare your successful habits to the ones you've struggled with, you'll likely find the times you've stumbled and veered off track are about the same. The big difference will be in how those stumbles line up over time.

If you commit to trying something new and forgiving yourself when you make a mistake, you'll see that when you mess up, you get right back to work. When it happens again, you do the same. Over time, your failures become fewer and further between.

But when you force yourself to be perfect from the outset, it's easy to lose motivation after just one stumble. One leads to two. Two leads to three. Pretty soon, you've given up entirely. The longer you veer off track, the easier it becomes to stay there.[11]

Here is the relevance for our teams: "when you force yourself to be perfect from the outset, it's easy to lose motivation after just one stumble. One leads to two. Two leads to three." If the goal of your play is *perfection*, then this is when we allow one error to devastate us. We failed, and there is no way to go back and fix it, nor is there any forgiving ourselves because we feel like that would be lowering our expectations.

Nonsense! Perfection is not only improbable, it just isn't realistic. Even so-called "perfect games" in baseball and softball have mistakes, missed pitches, poor at-bats. In over 140 years of Major League Baseball, over 210,000 games played, there have been 23 "perfect games" recorded. By professionals at the highest level!

When perfection is our expectation, then it is easy to lose our focus after one error or mistake. But when we forgive ourselves—and our teammates—and we have a routine to flush the memory of it away and refocus on the next pitch, then we are setting ourselves up to minimize mistakes. This is what championship teams have learned to do better than common teams. Everything else being even—talent, physical traits, effort—the team that has developed this skill will outlast and outperform the team that doesn't, 10 times out of 10.

I am so confident in the benefits of a strong mental game that I am willing to say it *guarantees* more success for teams that value it. Personally, when I began to understand this part of the game is when I felt like I was just beginning to learn what coaching is all about. It has truly been a difference-maker, not only for my teams, but for every aspect of my life.

PART III

THE PARENT

"Some people have to wait their entire lives to meet their favorite player. I raised mine."

17

WHAT REALLY MATTERS

When I look back at my own experience and the many car rides home from ballgames, I am disappointed with the way I handled a good number of those moments. If I can share what I have learned from my own failures, then perhaps it will help to create a better experience for other parents and young athletes who happen to read this.

Imagine you are driving home from your child's baseball game. What does it feel like in the car ride home when your child goes 4-for-4 in the game? I am guessing it is pretty positive. He feels good about himself. You feel very proud. You might even reward his great performance with ice cream or a milkshake. The team could have even lost the game, but deep down everyone in your car feels pretty good because of his 4-for-4 performance. And it is okay to feel good about it, I certainly do not want to belittle any of the joy that is felt from a job well-done.

But now let's flip the script. Imagine what it feels like in the car ride home when your child goes 0-for-4. I am guessing it is pretty quiet. If he is a competitor, he probably feels bad about himself. He may even be starting to question himself or starting to doubt his ability. Going 0-4 feels like the end of the world. He feels like he not only let himself down, but he let his team down, he let his coach down, and he let his family down.

Why does it feel that way? Why does he feel like he has let his family down?

Perhaps it is because we only celebrate success in terms of the number of base hits he gets? Or when he is pitching, by the number of strikeouts he records? Or when he is asked to play a different role that day (like being a substitute who comes off the bench), by the number of innings he was out on the field?

Why does the climate in the car ride home change so drastically because of these factors? I am not suggesting that we should all superficially act exactly the same after a player has had a bad game as we do when he or she has had a great game. I am not suggesting that it is even realistic to assume he or she won't feel bad after a rough game.

What I am suggesting is, perhaps we need to consider new criteria for success, and allow that to control the climate and the conversation in our car on the way home. For example, he may have gone 0-for-4 that day, but how did he react after striking out? Did he hustle back to the dugout and calmly put his helmet and bat down? How did he run out ground balls and popups? Did he sprint them out as hard as he could? How did he pick up his teammates throughout the game? Did he have good approaches to his at-bats?

Talk about those things. They are successes. They are things to celebrate. Set aside the common, numbers-based, measurements for success. Let the real criteria for the climate in the car ride home be: *how did he play the game?*

Those intangibles are what really matters, especially in the long run. Your child can't completely control whether or not he goes 0-for-4 or 4-for-4. But he *can* control *how hard he tries.*

Mom and Dad, that should be our only focus on the car ride home. Your child's attitude and your child's effort are so much more valuable than their stats. You can model this and teach it to them at a very young age by championing and celebrating those true measurements of success, regardless of whether or not they went 4-for-4 or 0-for-4, or whether or not they even got into the game. A positive attitude and being a good teammate are a primary part of the foundation upon which champions are built.

18
_____

I LOVE WATCHING YOU PLAY

Every dad and every mom are the first "coach" to their kids. Whether you wear the official hat or not and whether you stand in the coach's box or not, parents are their kids' first coaches. Maybe that is why we all have a tendency to want to *coach them up* during their athletic endeavors. Some of us do it during the game by shouting "coaching words" from wherever we are sitting, whether we are actually a coach on the team bench or whether we are sitting on the other side of the fence in the bleachers. Regardless, many of us often feel the need to voice some extra coaching advice while on the walk from the field to the parking lot, or while on the car ride home after the game.

I would be interested to know what percentage of moms and dads (dads in particular) actually do *not* do these things. I will bet it is less than 10%. I actually did meet a dad once who was part of the 10%. I was attending one of those large, showcase recruiting events with my son. While the players were on the field working out, I began a conversation with one of the fathers in the stands. Pretty early in our talk I could tell that he knew very little about baseball. Then he told me something that I found to be pretty fascinating.

He said, "I have no athletic bone in my body and I have never played a day of baseball in my life. But I have attended all of my son's games since he was little and I just love watching him play."

He went on to explain that he intentionally chose to *not* learn much about the game of baseball over the years because he felt like the more he knew about the game, the more expectations he would begin placing on his son, and he didn't want to take the enjoyment out of it for him. More importantly, he said, "The more I learned about the game, the more tempted I would be to begin shouting expectations from the stands. My son doesn't need that from me. He just needs me to be his biggest fan."

Wow! What an awesome perspective. Honestly, I had never heard of such perspective before, from any dad, ever in my whole life! I can only imagine what that must have been like for the kid as a young player. Growing up with a father who simply attended his games, watched him play, and never said a word except "Great job." No coaching him up from the stands. No shouting at umpires. No second-guessing coaches, starting lineups or decisions.

This whole idea triggered a rather interesting thought in my mind. Perhaps the less dad knows about baseball, the better the baseball experience can be for the child. Think about that for a second.

I don't believe that *has* to be the case and I don't believe it would be true in *all* cases. But imagine this. Picture an entire field of kids playing the game of baseball. Now imagine an entire bleacher section full of moms and dads who are exactly like that guy I met at the showcase. Imagine, during the game, three or four of those kids make an error. Another three or four of them strike out. The two players who pitch during the game walk four batters a piece, and their team loses the game. To make matters even worse, the ump was terrible.

How might the words coming from the bleachers be different? How might the post-game conversations from the field to the parking lot be different? How might the feelings that those children have toward the game of baseball be different afterwards? I wonder.

I don't think it's necessary for us moms and dads to have no knowledge of the game or any athletic interest in order for our kids to be able to enjoy playing it. However, I do think we can all learn a lot from parents who are like that dad I met.

It is so difficult to set aside the urge to want to constantly "coach up" your own kids. But we really need to try. Restraint is a discipline, and we need to build this discipline within ourselves. We need the discipline to make the choice to refrain from giving unnecessary coaching advice to our kids while they are trying to play the game.

Really, all most kids want to know from their parents is one thing. That *one thing* is something the dad at the showcase said to me: "I just love watching him play."

What if that was all we chose to say to our kids after their games? What if we never offered them a single bit of coaching advice (unless they asked us for it), but simply told them, "I love to watch you play."

Whether they went 3-for-4 or whether they struck out 4 times. "I love to watch you play."

Whether they started and played the entire game or whether they pinch hit for one at-bat. "I love to watch you play."

Whether they won or lost. "I love to watch you play."

I wonder what that would do for our relationships with our children?

Oh, and by the way, the son of that dad I met at the showcase, he went on to play ball in college. Imagine that! A dad who knew nothing about the game, offered no coaching advice to his son for 18 years, but was able to raise a son who was a great high school player and even played at the next level.

Remember that dad and his son, especially the next time you think it is so urgent for your 11-year old to hear from you exactly what he did wrong in his 20th game of the season this year.

19

A DIFFERENT PERSPECTIVE

Here is a little experiment for you to try. The next time you are on vacation or visiting a city in which you know few if any people, go find a ball park or a gym where there are youth games in progress and just sit back and watch. Not just the game, take notice of the entire scene. The fans, the parents, the players, the officials.

There are a few things you might notice:

- *The officials are fairer.* It is amazing how good the officials are when you have no stake in the game. Or, if the official does make a mistake, you might be surprised at how little temptation you have to shout at him or point it out. You might actually find yourself feeling some compassion for him.

- *Some of the parents sound ridiculous.* You will likely hear people shouting things at their kids that make you shake your head and think, "That poor kid. Leave him alone. Just let him play." It is amazing how different things sound when you don't know any of the people who are saying them.

- *You will forget about everything that happened in the game within hours.* There might be errors, bad pitches, bad passes, bad shots, and poor coaching decisions, but none of it really matters to you. Therefore, it will be easy to forget. Imagine if we had the ability to have that short a memory at our own kids' games?

This exercise has been good for me, personally. I love watching baseball, and so I will often find a game to watch. A couple years ago, while I was watching an 8U game where I knew no one, I noticed some of those things that I described, and it really made me think about the idea of *perspective*.

The perspective with which I was watching the game of strangers playing was one of no emotion. I had no feelings or emotion invested in the game, and honestly that felt pretty good. I was simply able to watch a game and not be emotionally caught up in the ups and downs. Doing so made me see the game a whole lot differently. I liked it. I liked the way it felt.

So, I began praying that I would be able to watch my own kids' games with less emotion. Of course, the emotions come from loving them so much and wanting to see them succeed. So, maybe to help us keep our emotions in check, we need to reconsider our expectations that we have placed on our children.

No parent feels like they are too hard on their kids. Everyone has justification for why they need to provide extra coaching points before and after a game. Some even say, "It's what my son wants. My daughter welcomes it. They *want* me to critique them."

Unfortunately, those who are guilty of this kind of behavior often do not recognize it in themselves until after their kids are all grown.

This is actually one of the reasons why I chose to write this book, with expectation that I might be able to help a few well-intentioned parents to not make the same mistakes that countless others who went before them have made.

Here is the truth. I don't care how competitive your kid is, rarely do they ever *really* want your constant critique. They just know that you are going to give it to them anyway. So, because they want to please you and get your approval, and because they know that you want them to want your critique, they acquiesce. They look like they are listening, but what is really going through their mind?

Sometimes when I talk to young kids about ballgames and their experiences while playing, I will ask them a multiple-choice question such as this: "What is your favorite thing for your mom and dad to do while they are watching you play?"

(A) Offer coaching advice
(B) Yell at the refs or umps
(C) Cheer for you
(D) None of the above; just sit quietly and watch

Which answer would you guess that I hear most often? If you said a combination of C and D you are correct. Guess which answer I have *never* heard, not one time, from any of the kids I have asked? Answer B.

No child enjoys hearing his parents yell at officials. Yet, guess what many parents spend 75% or more of their time doing at ballgames? Most of us are guilty, myself included. Still, we have the ability and the opportunity to *choose* to behave differently.

I have found it fascinating that some kids will even say answer D, that they would rather their parents sit quietly and say *nothing* at all during the games. I asked my own daughter this question during one of her high school basketball seasons and her first, instinctive answer was D. Then she followed it up with, "Well, I don't mind if you cheer for the team."

Because of the way she said that, I followed up with another question. I asked, "Which do you like better, when we cheer loud for *you* or when we cheer loud for the *team?*"

Without hesitation she said, "The team."

I have a suspicion that most kids would answer that question the same way. As parents and adults, we often are so focused on our own individual kids that we lose perspective of the greatest value of their athletic experience—the value of *team*. And guess what? Your children want you to love their team as much as they do. Your children want you to support their team as much as you support them. This is the perspective of champions.

20

DRINK FROM THE WATER HOSE KIDS

In 2014, Coach Tony Robichaux of the Louisiana-Lafayette Ragin' Cajuns baseball team made a lot of noise on many social media outlets when he made this statement regarding the kind of players he looks to recruit for the Ragin' Cajuns program: "We want guys who drink out of the water hose, not the guy whose mommy is bringing him a Powerade in the third inning."

Obviously, Coach Robichaux was speaking metaphorically, using an exaggerated statement that was meant to describe a general mindset, attitude, or ethic. It is *not* a statement about keeping kids hydrated or about consuming a beverage. If that is the only thing you see when you read that statement, then you are missing the point. Also, if you think his statement has anything to do with disrespecting mommies or daddies or being unappreciative of their love and devotion to their kids, neither is that the focus.

What is he saying? Here is what I think he is saying: kids who "drink from the water hose" very likely do not have helicopter parents. Water hose kids are those who, at an early age, know what uniform they are wearing in tomorrow's game and know how to put it on themselves; they know what all pieces of equipment they need for tomorrow's game and pack their equipment bag themselves; they carry their own equipment bag to and from the field themselves. I see *way* too many moms and dads dragging equipment bags these days!

Do "water hose" kids fail sometimes? Absolutely! Because they are allowed to! They may leave their glove in the dugout from time to time, because mom didn't come in and pack up their bag for them. What a great learning opportunity it can be for a child to experience that sinking feeling in his stomach because he got home and discovered his glove is not in his equipment bag. Time to problem-solve, another great life lesson! Too many kids are getting robbed of some very valuable life lessons because they are having too many responsibilities taken away from them.

Coach Robichaux was saying that he wanted to recruit kids who have the ability to survive on their own. Again, the metaphor is not about hydrating or drinking water, but the principle can certainly apply: they know when they need a drink, and when they need a drink they know how to find one. Why? Because not everything in their life has been handed to them. They have had to solve some problems on their own along the way.

Let me be clear, I know helicopter parenting happens because of the immense amount of love you feel for your child, and because of your great concern for their well-being. My wife and I have both fought it in many different circumstances we have been faced with while raising our kids. It is hard to not coddle. But we, as parents who love our kids more than we can possibly describe, have to figure out how to support them without pampering them. We have to be courageous enough to let them fail, and insightful enough to realize that great lessons and maturity come from failure.

Suppose you are a parent who comes into the dugout at the end of your child's game and helps them pack up their equipment and throw away their empty water bottles, and then you carry out their equipment bag and cooler for them. If so, here is a simple little step in the right direction for next game—*don't do it*.

What possible harm can befall your child by letting him pack up his own gear and carry it out to the car? It is actually quite the opposite. Your child will take a step toward understanding the virtue of taking *responsibility*, which brings all sorts of benefits along with it, such as being a good teammate, being a good person, developing good work ethic, developing confidence, developing toughness—which are all things we want to see them display on the playing field.

Ironically, we don't realize how much we can help them as a player *on the field* by consciously making an effort to *not* help them with so many little tasks *off the field*.

21

BEWARE OF GROUPTHINK

What is "groupthink?" Yes, it is an actual word. It is a word that was first used by social psychologist Irving Janis in 1972. Groupthink emerges whenever a group of people encourage the conformity of an opinion instead of trying to find the best solution. Irving Janis describes it like this: "groupthink occurs when a group makes faulty decisions because group pressures lead to a deterioration of mental efficiency, reality testing, and moral judgment."[12]

Group pressures lead to a deterioration of mental efficiency, reality testing, and moral judgment. This is fascinating to me. It is fascinating because I see it all the time. All it takes is one scroll down through your social media timeline and you will find it.

For example, suppose you are scrolling down through your Facebook timeline and you see a post that has collected a lot of comments. It piques your interest, and so you read the post. It says something like this:

My son's teacher has required all the students in her class to use yellow #2 lead pencils. We don't have any yellow #2 lead pencils at our house and so now we have to drive to the store to buy some. We have plenty of mechanical pencils, which is my son's pencil of choice. But NO, this teacher wants everyone to use a #2 lead pencil (and he said she sounded really mean when she told them this). Has anyone else had this teacher? Is this the kind of inconvenience I should expect from her all year? I feel like just sending him to school with the pencils we already have instead of going out to buy more pencils just because this one teacher has some specific affinity for a yellow #2 lead pencil.

Now, of course, this sounds like a silly example (it is meant to sound silly, because in reality many of the things we get so upset about on social media are silly). Yet, posts like these incite 20, 30, and sometimes more than 60 replies in the comment section. All sorts of people will jump on board to express their disdain for that particular teacher. Some share their own experiences. Some have never even met the teacher, but because they know and love the person who posted the original message, they support that parent by agreeing with how stupid the teacher is.

Then what happens is, after a number of affirming comments are made, the original poster feels justified and legitimized in their rant, regardless of how ridiculous it was or how inaccurate it was, or how damaging it was to the reputation of another.

Perhaps if the person who made the original post had the *mental efficiency* to actually *test the reality* of the situation before taking to social media, they would have found that the teacher *actually* told all the students that they would "need a yellow #2 lead pencil for some of the tests they will be taking throughout the year, and so you should go ahead and get some yellow #2 lead pencils to bring in and store in the classroom," which doesn't sound unreasonable or mean. Understanding the full and complete facts of any given situation certainly help us to make better *moral judgments* in how we respond to those situations.

Groupthink is harmful to people. It is ultimately, quite frankly, more harmful to those who participate in it, because they appear less trustworthy. It is hard to trust someone who doesn't think for themselves, who constantly seeks validation and affirmation from the "comment" section of their social media feeds.

As a coach, I have been the victim of the groupthink mentality more than once. A mom or a dad becomes frustrated because their son isn't playing as much as they feel he should (which is usually one of the main reasons for social media rants in the context of sports—their child's playing time). I understand the feeling, I really do. We love our kids. They are the only kids on that team that we see regularly at the dinner table, at bedtime, and in the mornings. We see their pain. We see their hard work and their determination. We see their discouragement whenever that hard work isn't rewarded with playing time. I get it.

But rather than speaking with our children about how to handle those kinds of disappointments with dignity, courage and honor, we too often resort to social media or other forms of gossip. Rather than encourage our children to use the experience as an opportunity to grow in their understanding of "team" and how to be the best teammate they can be even when things are not going their way, we instead complain within earshot of them about how angry we are at the coach. Perhaps some parents even tell their kids directly that their coach is an idiot for not playing them. Ultimately, way too many people seek to find solace and comfort from the groupthink tank.

Way too many coaches have been made to be a villain in social media posts over the years. They have been the subject of rants about how blind they are to not be able to see true talent and dedication, how unfair they are, how they show favoritism, and an onslaught of other accusations.

Then comes the groupthink. The comments start rolling in. People from all over the globe are all of a sudden experts at coaching, and they provide input on the coaching decisions of someone they have never even met. They may have never even seen a single game. They couldn't name any of the other players on the team. But they know for a fact that this particular coach must be an idiot because he disappointed their friends.

Beware of groupthink. It will dumb you down. Whenever a person gets lured into groupthink, they start limiting their own thinking and they ignore any alternative perspective. Irving Janis identified eight symptoms of groupthink. When these symptoms exist, there is a reasonable chance that groupthink is happening:[13]

1. *Illusion of invulnerability.* Groupthink creates excessive optimism that might be completely unfounded in reality.

2. *Collective rationalization.* Participants of groupthink discredit warnings to the contrary and do not reconsider their assumptions.

3. *Belief in inherent morality.* Participants in groupthink believe in the rightness of their cause and therefore ignore the ethical or moral consequences of their words or actions.

4. *Stereotyped views of out-groups.* Negative views of the "enemy" or the subject of the complaints make any effective responses to conflict seem unnecessary.

5. *Direct pressure on dissenters.* In the rare occasion that someone should bring up a contrasting view to the groupthink, they are quickly shot down.

6. *Self-censorship.* Any personal doubts or concerns one might have about the group consensus are oppressed rather than given consideration.

7. *Illusion of unanimity.* People who participate in groupthink often assume their views are shared among a majority of people, when in fact those opinions are just the loudest, and their groupthink is simply creating an illusion that it is the majority.

8. *Self-appointed mind-guards.* Participants in groupthink protect the group and the originator from information that is problematic or contradictory to the group's view, words and actions.

The affirmations and validation brought on by groupthink tend to lead to carelessness and irrational thinking, because the nature of the groupthink experience is a failure to consider all alternatives or other perspectives that could potentially make our opinions on the matter seem wrong or out of line. Ultimately, any decisions that are shaped by groupthink have low probability of achieving successful outcomes. Little good ever comes from groupthink.

Groupthink is a problem that has been around for as long as people have had social lives, but it is a lot easier to recognize in the days of social media, and if we are not careful it can easily grow out of control.

Beware of groupthink. Watch for it, and then ignore it. Choose to not participate. Encourage others to not participate. It is a harmful thing. It causes us to lose *mental efficiency*—we stop thinking for ourselves. We stop *reality testing*—we fail to test everyone's opinions with the reality of the situation. Ultimately, we end up lacking *moral judgment*—we make decisions based on others' judgment and moral character rather than our own discernment, research and convictions.

You be *you*. Think. Research. Pause before you speak. Don't just toss your issue out in the open and allow it to get caught in the whirlwind of groupthink. It rarely ever helps.

When you see it on your timeline, click away from it. Stop reading it. Don't participate. No good or positive result will ever come from complaining about your child's coach online. I can't think of a single time when any good has come from such behavior.

Maybe right now you are thinking, "I can tell you what good comes from it, *I feel better*. I have to have some place to vent my frustration, and that is as good a place as any. When people agree with me, it makes me feel better."

May I be candid? The "I just need to vent" justification is a pathetic reason to engage in groupthink rants. Think about it. You feel good by doing something that creates more negativity in the world? You feel good by saying something that negatively sways another person's opinion about a situation they know nothing about or their opinion of someone they have never even met?

Why are our *feelings* so important? I know sometimes life can be frustrating, but let's find more productive ways to "vent." Go for a walk. Go for a run. Go to the gym and toss around some weights. Go hit a punching bag.

Actually, a better way to confront negative feelings and the temptation to vent and go on rants that suck people into groupthink is *gratitude*. Before you start ranting, catch yourself. Force yourself to get up from your computer or to put down your phone. Go out for a walk and begin thinking about and saying out loud some of the things you are thankful for. It is very difficult to be a negative person when your heart is filled with gratitude. You will find that you have so much more to be thankful for than to complain about, and pretty soon your complaint will seem very small and trivial.

I pray about this. This issue is one that I pray for in the culture of youth sports. I love sports. I love coaches. I love players. I love parents. There is so much value in the experiences of youth sports. There are so many blessings and lessons that inspire lifelong success, which all come from the many different kinds of experiences of youth sports—both the positive experiences as well as the negative ones.

My prayer for every coach, player, and parent is that we will be intentional about getting just a little better every day in the practices and behaviors that we have discussed throughout this book. When you do, there is a possibility that you could win a championship, but that probably won't have anything to do with anything you read in this book. You may never win a championship. They are not guaranteed. I prefer to focus on things I can control, which is what every single chapter in this book has been about. You are not in control of whether or not you ever win a championship, but you are absolutely in control of whether or not you will be a champion. I pray that you will always play to win in what really matters!

EPILOGUE

Don't Blink, Coach-Dad

I was a coach before I was a dad. By the time we had our firstborn, I had been coaching baseball for five years. From the time I had stopped playing, I started coaching. I immediately fell in love with it, and felt like it was part of my calling in this world; something I would probably continue doing for as long as I could and perhaps one day I would get to coach my own children, if they loved the game and wanted to play. We assumed they would, but my wife and I committed to never force sports onto them.

After our son was born, he indeed did love playing ball. It seemed like that was all we did during his childhood. Then, a couple years later, we brought into this world a little girl and she started picking up the bats and balls and playing right beside her older brother. We quickly realized it was not going to be something we would need to convince our children to try to enjoy. It was inside of them just like it was inside me as early as I can remember. A love for the game.

When it was time to transition from playing in the backyard to playing on teams, I did indeed get to coach my kids, beginning with my son's 8U baseball team and then all the way through high school.

It was through baseball that he developed most of his friendships, and the majority of those friends continued to play together for the next 10-11 years. They played a lot of baseball together over the course of their childhood years, and they experienced a lot of *life* together simply because of a game—baseball.

Then, in what felt like the blink of an eye, one day they played their last game together. I remember that night and the way I felt long into the evening after that final game was over. I was sitting in a chair in our living room in silence and my son came upstairs and handed me a baseball. It was the home run ball he had hit in that final game, and he wanted me to have it. On the ball, he had written three inscriptions:

- 2-Run Homerun—I love you
- Last game as a Bulldog
- Thank you for being my mentor in life and in baseball

In my mind as I sat in the chair, just before he handed me the baseball, I was back in the yard and he was five years old. I blinked. And when I looked up he was an 18-year old man with a baseball in his hand. My boy.

It is not easy being a coach's kid. The spotlight—or crosshair—is on you at all times. Inevitably there are times when people feel disgruntlement toward the coach-dad and for some reason they subsequently project those feelings toward the player-son, either directly and openly or indirectly and privately. Even at home, the pressure and stress that coach-dad feels is sometimes difficult to suppress, which means player-son feels and takes on those burdens as well. The game becomes a completely different experience for that kid simply because he is the coach's kid, and that experience is not always a pleasant one.

I love all my players just like sons, but every father admittedly loves his own son a little differently, which then creates a very difficult dynamic to navigate in practices, games, and team activities. A friend of mine, who also coached his own son in high school once told me, "If you end up coaching your own son one day you just hope he is either A) head and shoulders more talented than the other players and there is no question about his playing time because he is obviously going to be a draft pick someday, or B) really terrible and unskilled, to the point where he is just happy to be on the team, and everyone including him knows there is no expectation of ever getting into the game. If your own son is in one of those two categories it is fairly easy to coach your own son. However, most coach's kids are in category C) good player, but has to work hard like everyone else to compete for a spot. This is the toughest situation for the coach's child, because no matter what he does it will not be good enough in many people's minds and if he earns a starting spot on the team it will obviously be, in many people's minds, due to being favored because he is the coach's kid.

This is the category most coach's kids fall under. It is where my son was. He worked his butt off, and at times when he started to relax a little bit, I would remind him that he needed to give a little more than everyone else. It probably wasn't fair to him, but I hope it is something he will look back on and appreciate. Even more, something he will learn from and reflect on as he one day raises his own family.

As an adult man before I had children, I can't remember a single time when I had cried openly, with tears. I had emotions, but I was never an *emotional* person. Things didn't touch me or move me emotionally in the way they began to after children were brought into the picture. It was a weird feeling for this macho guy. I remember standing above the baby cribs of both my children and not being able to control the flood that filled my eyes. I knew, in those moments, that things for me would never be the same. I remember praying that they would always love Jesus, and still do pray that prayer. When I stood over my toddler son's bed at night while he slept, I prayed that I would be the kind of mentor and role model he would need in life, and that I would have the opportunity to one day be his coach.

It happened. And then it was over. In a blink, it seems.

I have a lot of baseballs. Over the years I collected balls that I hit over the fence as a little leaguer, game balls from big wins I pitched in high school and in college, game balls from big wins in coaching, signed balls from players and teams I have coached, league championship balls, district championship balls, balls that are autographed by pros like Cal Ripken Jr.—I have a lot of baseballs sitting around my house and office.

None of those compare to the one ball that was handed to me in my living room late one evening after my son's and my final game together. This one ball tells a big story. It tells the story of this entire book. It reveals answers to prayers that I prayed while standing over a baby crib many years ago. And on it is the signature of my favorite baseball player in all the world.

NOTES

1 **According to an Open Access Journal of Sports Medicine study:** Merkel, Donna. "Youth Sport: Positive and Negative Impact on Young Athletes", May 31, 2013. https://www.ncbi.nlm.nih.gov/pmc/articles/PMC3871410.

2 **Former NFL 1ˢᵗ Round draft pick:** Eades, John. "What You Do Shouldn't Define You With Perry Tuttle", April 25, 2017. http://followmylead.libsyn.com/what-you-do-shouldnt-define-you-with-perry-tuttle.

3 **I once read about how in Japanese culture:** Tugend, Alina. *Better by Mistake*, 2012.

4 **Jon Gordon wrote a really great book:** Gordon, Jon. *The Positive Dog*, 2012.

5 **Skip Bertman, the legendary coach from LSU:** Cain, Brian. "5X NCAA Nation Champion's Advice For You". https://briancain.com/blog/5x-ncaa-national-champions-advice-for-you.html.

6 **You say that you want:** Ferraro, Joe. "Episode 5: Mike Rooney-The Power of Perseverance", July 23, 2017. http://onepercentbetterpodcast.libsyn.com/episode-5-mike-rooney-the-power-of-perseverance.

7 **What does the life you want require:** Kight, Tim & Brian. "#02: Discipline Over Default", January 30, 2017. http://focus3.libsyn.com/02-discipline-over-default.

8 **When we talk about the mental game:** Cain, Brian. "BC 134. Dave Hilton | Mental Game Lessons from Playing & Coaching in Pro Baseball", May 17, 2017. https://briancain.com/blog/bc-134-dave-hilton-mental-game-lessons-from-playing-coaching-in-pro-baseball.html.

9 **Anyone who says failure is not an option:** "Goodreads Inc.". https://www.goodreads.com/quotes/961471-anyone-who-says-failure-is-not-an-option-has-also.

10 **It is a mental strength routine:** This routine was adapted from Brian Cain's 4RIP3 Mental Conditioning Program as explained in his DVDs and videos, which can be found at: "Championship Productions", 2012. http://www.championshipproductions.com/cgi-bin/champ/p/Baseball/4RIP3-A-Mental-Conditioning-Program-for-Baseball_LD-04093B.html?id=yEaSbPL36p6a.

11 **I don't claim to have all the answers:** Tervooren, Tyler. "Forget Perfection, Just Don't Fail Twice In A Row". https://www.riskology.co/forget-perfection.

12 **Groupthink emerges whenever:** "Psychologists for Social Responsibility". http://www.psysr.org/about/pubs_resources/groupthink%20overview.htm.

13 **Irving Janis identified eight symptoms of groupthink:** Ibid.